The Joan Palevsky  Imprint in Classical Literature

In honor of beloved Virgil—

"O degli altri poeti onore e lume . . ."

—Dante, *Inferno*

The publisher gratefully acknowledges the generous support of the Classical Literature Endowment Fund of the University of California Press Foundation, which was established by a major gift from Joan Palevsky.

Ancient Greek Epigrams

Ancient Greek Epigrams

Major Poets in Verse Translation

Gordon L. Fain

UNIVERSITY OF CALIFORNIA PRESS

Berkeley   Los Angeles   London

University of California Press, one of the most distinguished
university presses in the United States, enriches lives around the
world by advancing scholarship in the humanities, social sciences,
and natural sciences. Its activities are supported by the UC Press
Foundation and by philanthropic contributions from individuals
and institutions. For more information, visit www.ucpress.edu.

University of California Press
Berkeley and Los Angeles, California

University of California Press, Ltd.
London, England

Illustrations by Margery J. Fain

Library of Congress Cataloging-in-Publication Data

   Ancient Greek epigrams : major poets in verse translation /
Gordon L. Fain.
     p.   cm.
   Includes bibliographical references and index.
   ISBN 978-0-520-26579-0 (cloth : alk. paper)
   ISBN 978-0-520-26580-6 (pbk. : alk. paper)
   1. Epigrams, Greek—Translations into English.   2. Greek
poetry—Translations into English.   I. Fain, Gordon L.
   PA3623.A5F35   2010
   881'.0108—dc22   2009042975

Manufactured in the United States of America

19 18 17 16 15 14 13 12 11 10
10 9 8 7 6 5 4 3 2 1

This book is printed on Cascades Enviro 100, a 100% post
consumer waste, recycled, de-inked fiber. FSC recycled certified
and processed chlorine free. It is acid free, Ecologo certified, and
manufactured by BioGas energy.

To the late Guy Lee and the late John Crook,
both of St. John's College, Cambridge,
both born on Guy Fawkes Day

ἔλαμψαν δ' ἀελίου δέμας ὅπως
ἀγλαὸν ἐς φάος ἰόντες δίδυμοι

Pindar, Pae. 12, fr. 52m

CONTENTS

PREFACE

The epigrams of the ancient Greeks had an enormous influence on Latin and later European poetry and are familiar to scholars, but they are not very well known to the general reader. Part of the reason is that editions of Greek epigrams in translation often include too many poems of too many poets. Anyone who peruses the more than four thousand epigrams in the Loeb *Greek Anthology* is likely to be quickly discouraged. Many of the poems are difficult to understand without some explanation, and the majority are not very good. The best are among the finest poetry the Greeks ever wrote, but finding them is not a task for the faint of heart.

For this reason I have assembled an anthology containing what I believe to be the most interesting poems of the most accomplished authors, with an introduction to the poetry and poets and with explanatory notes that place each epigram in context. Since this is a book for the general reader, I do not give the Greek texts, and there are no footnotes. The general reader is unlikely to be aided by extensive citations of the secondary literature, and scholars should be able to follow my arguments without them. I provide a selected bibliography of books and articles including those mentioned in the text, emphasizing works the general reader might find interesting. I give only a small fraction of the literature I have consulted in making my translations and writing the notes, and I extend my apologies to colleagues whose publications have not been specifically mentioned.

I am greatly indebted to the Helen Riaboff Whiteley Center at Friday Harbor, Washington, where most of the translations were done, and to Churchill College, Cambridge, where the introductory chapter was written and the book finished. I am also indebted to David Blank, who read chapter 9; to Michael Haslam, who read the whole of the manuscript and helped with the proofs; and to the anonymous referees of University of California Press. The text has greatly profited from their many corrections and perceptive suggestions. The press was enormously helpful at every stage in the preparation of the book, and I am particularly grateful to the copy editor, Alice Falk. My greatest debt is to my wife, Margery, who did the illustrations, read all of the text in several drafts, made innumerable helpful recommendations, and provided the love and support during the writing of the book that made it possible for me to complete it.

CHAPTER ONE

Introduction to Ancient Greek Epigrams

When we think of an epigram, we think of a short, witty poem with a
clever ending. The ancient Greeks had a very different conception.
Epigrams to them were verses written on something, as the word implies.
At least initially, they were poems engraved on tombstones or monuments,
or on statues or other offerings to the gods. Many of these inscriptions
have survived to the present day in ancient shrines and cemeteries. Like
inscriptions on our own memorials and gravestones, they are forthright
expressions of patriotism or personal sentiment, sometimes moving but
often formulaic and usually short, occasionally consisting of a single line.

Prompted by these poems written with some practical aim in view, the Greek poets of the third century BCE composed literary epigrams intended not to be inscribed but to be recited and published. Many of these poems were also epitaphs and dedications to gods, at first closely patterned on poems any literate Greek could have read in a temple or by the side of a village road. The poets then began to play with the form of actual inscriptions in clever and amusing poems of great variety. They expanded the range of epitaphs to include, for example, poems about dolphins washed ashore and lying dead on the beach. They wrote fictive inscriptions for fishermen or for elderly women who spun thread for a daily wage, who normally would be too poor to afford a grave marker. At about the same time, Greek poets also began to write epigrams about love. These charming poems are less closely related to inscriptions and probably emerged from the tradition of short songs and verses sung or recited at drinking parties. Greek love epigrams had an immense influence on Latin poets—notably on Catullus, who also wrote love epigrams, and on Propertius and Ovid, who wrote love elegies closely related to the Greek poems in style and theme. Then, much later, at the time of the Roman emperor Nero, the Greek poet Lucillius abandoned epitaphs, love, and practically everything else in favor of satirical epigrams with clever endings. The poems Lucillius wrote provided the thematic models for the Latin poet Martial, whose snappy verse with "point" established the epigram in the form it still has today.

The development of the Greek literary epigram is such a strange phenomenon, and these poems are so different from anything else in our tradition, that we are surprised and uncertain when we first encounter them. Why would anyone want to write a fictitious epitaph or dedication to a god? Why write love poems as epigrams and not as lyric poems like those of Sappho? Who were the Greeks of the third century BCE, and what forces in their tradition and society led them to express themselves in this particular way?

The short answer to these questions is that the Greeks who wrote literary epigrams were much like us, acutely aware of the great masters who came before them, excited by the many possibilities offered to them by their literary heritage, but nearly overwhelmed by the weight of tradition. Every schoolboy knew Homer, and many poets and scholars could recite much of the *Iliad* and *Odyssey* from memory. Like contemporary composers who sense Bach, Beethoven, and Brahms looming over their shoulders, Hellenistic Greek poets did not attempt to compete with their predecessors directly but sought alternative means of expression by altering old forms, inventing new genres, and merging one genre with another. From this impetus arose not only the literary epigram but also short comic poems called mimes, mini-epics we now call epyllia, and the whole tradition of pastoral poetry.

That is the short answer. For the long answer, I need to say more about Hellenistic Greek culture, which encouraged and nurtured this peculiar art form. I must then explore in greater detail the poems that were actually inscribed, which provided the stimulus for the development of their literary counterparts. This will help us see how simple expressions engraved on stone were turned into literature of a high order. I next review the tradition of lyric verse, drinking songs, and short elegy from which love epigrams emerged, in order to develop an appreciation for the Greek practice of *variatio,* of taking a theme or mode of expression from one poem and turning it into something subtly different. Then, after a few words about texts and method of translation, I turn to the poets and poems themselves.

HELLENISTIC GREECE

When Alexander the Great suddenly died in 323 BCE after twelve years of nearly constant warfare, he left behind an empire stretching from Greece and northern Africa through present-day Syria, Israel, Lebanon, and Jordan, including some or all of Turkey, Iraq, Iran, Afghanistan, Pakistan, and northern India. Since Alexander left no suitable heir, his conquered territory rapidly splintered into several parts, initially controlled by generals in Alexander's army. After much warfare, Greek rule was consolidated into three main kingdoms: one centered in Macedonia, Alexander's home in northern Greece; a second in eastern Asia, by far the largest of the three but the least stable; and the third in Egypt and North Africa, the richest and most long-lasting of the kingdoms, under the rule of Ptolemy I Soter ("Savior" or "Deliverer") and his successors.

For much of the next two centuries, the kingdom of the Ptolemies in Egypt became the most important center of Greek culture. Its capital was the great city of Alexandria near the westernmost confluence of the Nile River and Mediterranean Sea. Alexander the Great is reputed to have personally laid out the main thoroughfares and walls of the city, and the Ptolemies built magnificent courtyards and palaces, creating the most sumptuous and populous city of the ancient world until Rome under Augustus. Alexandria was strategically placed to export manufactured goods and import grain, carrying on brisk trade with Egypt and principalities throughout the Mediterranean. Alexandria itself manufactured glass, pottery, perfumes, and papyrus from raw materials coming from the Nile Delta and as far away as India. Strabo, a Greek historian and geographer whose life spanned the first centuries BCE and CE, claimed that Alexandria was the largest commercial center of the inhabited world. To this city came Greeks from the Greek mainland as well as from Greek islands and colonies as distant as Sicily and southern Italy. Many Egyptians and foreign immigrants from neighboring Palestine and Syria also came to establish businesses or look for work.

Alexandria was not only an important economic center but also a meeting place of artists and a focus of cultural life during the Hellenistic period. Among its immigrants were scholars and poets, including Theocritus from Sicily, Posidippus from Pella in Macedonia, and Callimachus from Cyrene in Libya. The islands of Kos and Samos also contributed many leading figures in literature and science, attracted in part by the wealth and refinement of the Ptolemies, who at least at the beginning of the dynasty were men of considerable learning. Ptolemy I wrote a history of the campaigns of Alexander the Great, and Ptolemy IV composed a tragedy called *Adonis* and founded a temple and cult of

Homer in Alexandria. The cultural influence of Alexandria spread far and wide throughout Hellenistic Greece, so that even poets and sculptors who never inhabited or even visited Alexandria were influenced by the spirit and energy radiating from the capital city.

During this period, the Ptolemies became the most important patrons of art and literature in the ancient world. The center of their patronage was the Museum dedicated to the Muses; established probably by Ptolemy I and situated near the royal palace, it provided offices and a large dining hall so that men of learning could take meals together, much as in a college today at Cambridge or Oxford. The Ptolemies also established a royal library, which eventually came to house nearly 500,000 book scrolls, the largest collection in the ancient world. Galen tells us that the Ptolemies were so eager to acquire books that they issued a decree saying that any scroll found on a ship docking in Alexandria must be seized and copied, with the original kept in the library and the copy given back to the owner.

The Museum and royal library became the nucleus of much of the intellectual activity of Ptolemaic Egypt. Although there is little direct evidence indicating exactly which branches of research were pursued, we can be confident that they included mathematics and science, as well as philological studies of ancient texts. The scholars of the Museum are known to have made essential contributions to organizing and editing the principal works of Greek literature; for example, they established the texts of the great Athenian tragedies in much the form we have them today. Eratosthenes of Cyrene, who held the position of head librarian of the royal library, wrote poetry and criticism of Greek comedy, but he was also an accomplished mathematician, a colleague of Archimedes, and the first to provide a reasonably accurate calculation of the circumference of the earth. He typifies the diversity of interests and intellectual achievements of Hellenistic Greece.

We now take for granted ready access to inexpensive and mass-produced paperbacks, as well as our huge research libraries where even rare books are easily consulted. In the ancient world, books were an uncommon and expensive commodity. It must have been a heady experience to budding Greek poets to have at their fingertips so much of the literature of preceding centuries, and their familiarity with this earlier poetry must have provided an enormous stimulus to their creativity. But the fascination of the Alexandrians with collecting and editing Greek literature also created its own particular burden. Homer came to be worshipped almost as a god, whose epics were so masterful they seemed beyond the reach of mortal poets. Even the best lyric verse of the day would inevitably evoke comparison with Sappho and Alcaeus, whose poems had been collected by Hellenistic scholars and made readily available. Little wonder that poets of the third century sought to escape direct comparison with their predecessors by exploring new forms of expression, modifying old genres, and inventing new ones.

We do not know why poets at the beginning of the third century BCE became so preoccupied with inscriptions and began to experiment with literary epitaphs and dedications. In his important book *Epigramm und Skolion,* the German scholar Richard Reitzenstein speculated that inscriptions from monuments and tombstones were at some point in the late fourth century BCE collected into books, which then made their way to Alexandria and other cities in the Greek empire. The first poets may have seen these poems and attempted to emulate them, attracted by their brevity and novelty.

It is equally possible, however, that the inspiration came from reading the inscriptions themselves. Anyte, among the first of the poets to create literary epigrams, probably began to write her poems before the establishment of the Museum and royal library, and there is no indication that she ever lived in Alexandria. She wrote many epitaphs for young girls and may have been inspired to write these poems because she had lost a friend or had been asked by an acquaintance to provide an epitaph. She also wrote epigrams about pets and other animals, subjects that begin to show up with some frequency in sculpture and painting during this period. At about the same time or perhaps a bit later, Leonidas of Tarentum adopted many of the themes of Anyte but extended the range of fictitious inscriptions to include epitaphs for people of the lowest social classes, who would not ordinarily have been able to afford a tombstone. Poor men and women also began to appear in Hellenistic sculpture—for example, in the statue of a toil-worn fisherman now in the Louvre, or the marble figure now in Munich of a drunken old woman clutching a wine flagon. Both Anyte and Leonidas included rural themes in their poetry, reflecting a new interest in the countryside among the city dwellers of Hellenistic Greece, also apparent in the landscape painting of this era and in the longer bucolic *Idylls* of Theocritus.

GREEK INSCRIPTIONS

The models for literary epitaphs and dedications composed during the third century BCE were actual verse inscriptions, which provided the themes and conventions that poets used in their verse. When the Greeks adopted from the Phoenicians most of the letters of the alphabet near the beginning or middle of the eighth century BCE, they also adopted the Phoenician practice of using these letters to inscribe monuments, grave-stones, and other objects. Phoenician inscriptions often consisted of one or a few words in prose, indicating the name of the person buried or the ownership of the object. Some of the earliest Greek inscriptions were like this too, but almost from the beginning the Greeks started to put inscriptions into verse. The most famous of the inscribed poems were the ones placed on monuments recording important events in Greek history, like those for the battles of Marathon and Thermopylae. These poems, many attributed to the sixth-century BCE Greek poet Simonides, must have been known to the first poets of literary epigrams, but they had less influence on the development of the subjects and style of Hellenistic verse than did the intimate poems inscribed on a statue in a shrine or on a tombstone in a country graveyard.

Some of the earliest surviving inscriptions were dedications to a god or goddess made in gratitude or in fulfillment of a vow or tithe. When warriors won a battle or farmers had a good harvest, they put some part of the spoils of victory or the first fruits of their fields into a shrine. They might also dedicate a statue or some other precious object *before* the battle or harvest, to propitiate the gods and win their favor. The offering was often accompanied by an inscription giving the name of the person making the dedication, the god to whom the dedication was made, and the purpose of the dedication. It was common for these inscriptions also to ask for something in return, though exactly what the god was supposed to provide was rarely stated explicitly.

One of the earliest of these poems (*CEG* 326, FH 35), from 700–675 BCE, was inscribed on the legs of a small bronze statue, which was discovered in Thebes and is now in the Boston Museum of Fine Arts. It says simply:

> Mántiklos has dedicated to
> The far-shooter of the silver bow
> Me as his tithe. So, Phoebus, now may you
> Some pleasing recompense bestow!

As was customary, the poem has the name of the dedicator (Mantiklos), the god to whom the statue was given (Phoebus—that is, Apollo), the reason for the dedication (as a tithe), and a polite request for something nice in repayment. The left hand of the statue seems to have held a bow, and Mantiklos may have been a successful warrior who had a statue of himself or of Apollo forged from the bronze of the spoils of battle. As in many early inscriptions, the object dedicated is in the first person. Visitors to the shrine may have stopped before the statue and enunciated the inscription, so that the statue would have seemed to be speaking.

Many of these same features are also present in another ancient inscription found on the thigh of a statue at Olympia, seen by Pausanias in the second century CE and included in his *Description of Greece* (5.27.12):

> The men of Mende dedicated me
> In this place, as first fruits of victory,
> To Zeus, king of the gods, when by their hand
> They overcame with force the Siptian land.

The circumstances of this statue and poem appear to have been quite similar to those of the Mantiklos inscription. The statue again was dedicated by warriors, though to Zeus instead of to Apollo, and again it would seemingly have spoken as the epigram was read.

The Hellenistic poet Asclepiades used similar conventions in the following dedication of a comic mask (GP 27, *AP* 6.308):

> Once Kónnaros wrote such a pretty hand,
> He vanquished all the other schoolboys, and
> > Got eighty knucklebones as prize.
> Then me, gift to the Muses, he hung here,
> A comic mask of old man Chares, near
> > The other children's claps and cries.

We have all the ingredients of an actual dedication inscription, and the voice of the poem is again the object of the dedication (a comic mask). Asclepiades used these conventions to write an amusing poem about a schoolchild who, instead of prevailing against a foreign army in a life-or-death struggle, overcame his other schoolmates and won a prize for penmanship. Knucklebones (often from sheep) were used like dice in children's games.

A dedication also speaks in this poem of Callimachus, who was probably born in the generation after Asclepiades (GP 25, *AP* 6.149):

> Euaínetos has dedicated me,
> A bronze cock, in return for victory
> > (At least he says it's so,
> > I wouldn't really know)
> To Castor and to Pollux, and I must
> Place in the son of Phaidros all my trust.

Here again are the components of an actual inscription; the "victory" mentioned in the poem was presumably that of a cockfight. The bronze rooster appears to be speaking just as in the other poems, but he surprises us by admitting he can't really vouch for the truth of anything he is saying, and that we have to take everything on the word of Euainetos. A passerby reading an actual inscription would not ordinarily question its veracity; that would have been taken for granted. By denying any responsibility for the truth of what he is saying, the cock confronts our expectations and calls into question the very essence of the convention. Callimachus in this poem provides a clever reflection upon the genre of the epigram itself, much as Pirandello does for theater more than two millennia later in *Six Characters in Search of an Author.*

The Greeks also followed the Phoenician practice of placing inscriptions on tombstones. These epitaphs resemble our own, providing essential information about the person buried and often a few words of commiseration or praise of the deceased. One of the very earliest surviving Greek epitaphs (*CEG* 132, FH 2) is on a limestone stele (a stone slab) from Corinth and dates from some time in the seventh century BCE. It says in a single line of verse:

This is the tombstone of Deinías, whom the shameless sea destroyed.

The voice of the epitaph belongs to the tomb or tombstone, which addresses the passerby in much the same way as do the dedications above, though in the third person rather than the first. Another early inscription dating from the middle or second half of the sixth century is similar (*CEG* 27, FH 82):

Stand near the grave of Kroísos, who is dead;
    Take pity on him, who once led
In battle with the champions, and whom
    Fierce Ares laid low in this tomb.

The poem begins with two imperatives addressed to the passerby; Ares is the god of war and the agent of death in battle. The epitaph could have been erected by Kroisos's father, but it is just as likely to have been put up by a grateful city for a brave young man who died in battle.

The poets of the third century BCE played with the conventions of epitaphs in much the same way they did for dedications. Here is a poem of Asclepiades (GP 31, *AP* 7.500), also with imperatives as in the epitaph for Kroisos, and also addressing the reader:

> Oh you, my empty barrow who pass by,
> When next in Chios, tell my father I
> Was wracked by storm, of ship and goods bereft,
> And only Eúhippos, my name, is left.

The epitaph seems to speak to us as we read it, but the voice of the poem comes not from the tombstone but rather from Euhippos, a merchant lost at sea. But it can't be coming from Euhippos either, at least not from his remains, since the poem begins by saying that the tomb is empty, presumably because Euhippos drowned and his body was never recovered. As we continue to read, the voice of the poem seems gradually to disappear like the Cheshire cat, leaving us with only a name. This is the sort of pleasantry the Hellenistic poets adored. Callimachus carried the game even further. The voice of the poem in his epitaphs often comes from the passerby, and in a few poems the passerby proceeds to strike up a conversation with the tombstone or deceased. Needless to say, none of this could possibly have been part of an inscription on an actual grave marker; it was rather an expression of the proclivity of Hellenistic poets to seem to adopt the conventions of inscriptions and then to extend those conventions in some novel and surprising direction.

Most epitaphs give essential information about the deceased, such as their name and patronymic and often the city or country from which they came. The Hellenistic poet Posidippus played with this expectation in two epigrams that appear one after the other in the recently discovered Milan papyrus. In both poems the voice comes from the dead person, who addresses the passerby. Instead of providing the usual information, however, the first poem (AB 102) complains about the necessity of doing so:

Why have you stopped, won't let me sleep,
And, standing near my gravestone, keep
On asking from what land I came,
And who's my father, what's my name?

In the second poem (AB 103), the complaint is just the opposite:

You don't ask where, from whom, or who
I am, as you're supposed to do,
But pass on by.

Both poems then proceed to give the name and patronymic of the deceased and his country of origin, thereby satisfying the requirements of the genre but in a way that is novel and unconventional.

The earliest actual inscriptions are mostly for men, and a large fraction are for warriors who died in battle. As time progressed, memorials to women became more common, especially to those who died in childbirth or before marriage. Many inscriptions of this kind have been discovered from the fourth century BCE, like this one (*CEG* 611) on a marble tombstone from Attica near Athens:

This earth, which covers you within its womb,
May now, Timókleia, above you lie,
But time can't touch your virtue, since this tomb
Records your chastity and will not die.

Markers of this sort were often erected by a family to provide some record of the life of a daughter who died too soon to leave a husband or child. As in many such inscriptions, the voice of the poem seems to come from an unspecified person probably meant to represent a member of the family or community, who directly addresses the young woman who has been buried.

Here is a very similar poem of the Hellenistic poet Anyte (GP 8, *AP* 7.649):

In place of wedding songs and bridal room,
Your mother set upon the marble tomb
A maiden with your grace and form instead,
So, Thérsis, we could greet you though you're dead.

This poem is in fact so similar in theme and format to the previous poem
that we can imagine it to have been engraved on a tombstone, though it
is a bit odd that the name of the mother isn't given. Whether written as
an actual inscription or as consolation to the family, it is a serious poem
with a mournful theme and quite different from the following epigram
by Leonidas of Tarentum, also of a woman and also with a statue on top
of the grave. But Leonidas's poem couldn't possibly have been written on
a real tombstone and is in fact one of the very few satirical epitaphs we
have from the third century (GP 68, *AP* 7.455):

Here Maronís, wine-lover, lies,
Mere ashes made of wine jars she drank up;
   And everyone can recognize
Above her tomb an Attic drinking cup.

   She does not mourn, below the earth,
The sons and husband now of her bereft,
   To whom she gave a life of dearth,
But this: that in the cup there's nothing left.

Dedication epigrams and epitaphs make up a large fraction of the poems
of Hellenistic poets, but these were not the only sort of epigrams they wrote.
Although we have only a small number of poems from each poet, pre-
served by anthologists with definite preferences for certain kinds of subject
matter, there are nevertheless examples of epigrams of many different sorts.
Even Anyte, one of the very first of the Hellenistic poets, wrote epigrams
that seem to be purely descriptive, perhaps intended to accompany a work
of art, and similar poems were also composed at about the same time or not
much later by Leonidas of Tarentum. For the third-century poet Posidippus
we are fortunate to have the recently discovered Milan papyrus, which con-

tains perhaps half of a book of poems apparently all by the same author (see the introduction to chapter 5). Together with epitaphs and dedications, there are poems on horse racing, gemstones, prognostication, and miraculous cures. We can only imagine what other themes would have been present if the whole of this book scroll of Posidippus had been preserved.

LOVE EPIGRAMS

Even further removed from the tradition of inscriptions are the poems about love, which are among the most interesting and enjoyable of all Hellenistic verses. They share with epitaphs and dedications a predilection for conciseness and brevity, but they emerged from a rather different lineage, that of short songs or poems sung or recited at a symposium. The Greek word *symposion,* which gave rise to the Latin *symposium,* is derived from a verb meaning "to drink together." Our view of a symposium is colored by the description in Plato of philosophers giving noble speeches on a common theme, but the beginning of his *Symposium* makes clear that the party Plato describes was meant to be something special. Most symposia were occasions for drinking and sex. Men came together in the evening with garlands in their hair and reclined at couches to eat and drink wine, often accompanied by adolescent boys and entertained by young girls who danced and played the flute. In the middle of the feasting, the men sang drinking songs called *skolia* or recited other short poems. Participants often took turns; a singer would hold a branch of myrtle or laurel and could stop at any point, even in the middle of a song. The sprig would then be passed to the next person, who would continue the song or begin something new.

The themes of the drinking songs were quite varied, but they were mostly short homilies with words of advice, or poems about wine and love. Here, for example, are two songs among the many *skolia* preserved by Athenaeus in his book *Deipnosophistae,* or *Scholars at Dinner* (15.694–96). Athenaeus wrote this treatise sometime near the end of the second or beginning of the third century CE, but the poems themselves are much older, perhaps dating from as early as the sixth century BCE:

If only it were possible to see
What sort of person everyone would be
By opening his chest, so we'd explore
What's in his soul, then close him up once more!
In this way we could tell our friends apart,
As those who have an undeceitful heart.

If only I could be
A great new pretty golden bowl,
And a pretty maid would carry me
With pure thoughts in her soul!

Among the lyric poets, Anacreon probably had the greatest influence on the development of Hellenistic love epigram. His verse, like that of many of the other archaic poets, has survived mostly from papyri or as fragments cited by other authors, but enough remains to give us a fair notion of his themes and style. The *Suda,* a tenth-century CE Byzantine encyclopedia, says that Anacreon's life was devoted to lyric poetry and to the love of women and boys. When asked why he did not write hymns to the gods, he reportedly replied that boys *were* his gods. He also had a reputation in antiquity for drunkenness, reflected in the poems the third-century poets wrote about him (see Leonidas XXIV). This combination of love and drink would have made his poetry a perfect entertainment at a symposium. The fragments of poems that are extant reveal a simplicity of expression and a seductive charm that explain his enormous popularity among the ancient Greeks, who erected a statue of him on the Acropolis in Athens showing him singing under the obvious influence of too much wine. Here are two representative selections of his verse, also cited in the *Deipnosophistae* of Athenaeus (13.564d, 10.475c):

Oh boy with girlish glance, I look for you,
But you don't notice me, and do
Not know that you control
The reins of my soul.

Come, let's not drink again as Scythians do,
No longer pandemonium and tumult raise,
But let's slow down, have only one or two,
And with our wine sing lovely songs of praise.

As important as the *skolia* and lyric poems were for the development of Hellenistic love poetry, collections of short poems in elegiac couplets may have been even more influential. The elegiac meter was the most common meter of inscriptions and literary epigrams, and I describe it in some detail later in the chapter. The only text of short elegiac poems that has come down to us is a book attributed to the poet Theognis. The *Suda* says that Theognis lived in the sixth century and was from Megara in Sicily, but there is good reason to believe he may have been born nearly a hundred years earlier in a different Megara—the one on the Greek mainland about halfway between Athens and Corinth. His poetry was well-known among educated Greeks in the fourth century and was cited by both Plato and Xenophon, so it is very likely to have been also widely available in the third century to the Hellenistic poets writing epigrams.

The text we have of Theognis is a hodgepodge of fragments and complete poems, probably mostly by Theognis himself but containing verses by other poets as well. Much of the poetry addresses a young man whose name was Kyrnos, whom the poet purports to be instructing in the ways of the world. It was common and viewed as customary to bring to a symposium a handsome adolescent who could be an *eromenos* or lover in a pederastic relationship. The boy would be introduced to the society of influential males and helped to find his place in society. Many of the poems or fragments of poems in the Theognis collection addressed to Kyrnos sound rather like Polonius's advice to his son. Here are two examples (lines 299–300, 457–60):

No man desires to be
A friend with you in time of doom,
    Though even, Kýrnos, he
Would have been born from the same womb.

A young wife's not good for a man who's old.
She's like a boat steered left that veers to right,
Breaks mooring lines, whose anchors do not hold,
And often finds another port at night.

In addition to homilies, the Theognis text also contains poems about love. In the version of Theognis that we have, most of the love poems are placed at the end in a separate book. Many scholars believe that the amatory verses were originally interspersed among the rest of the Theognis text but later were separated and put together at the end, perhaps to make them less easily available to young readers. Other scholars think that the second book was a separate collection and was never part of the original Theognis text. Nearly everyone agrees, however, that the amatory poetry, like the rest of the collection, dates at least from the third century BCE and was available to the Hellenistic poets. It could therefore have had a particularly important influence on the development of the love epigram.

Here are some representative excerpts from the amatory verses in the second book of Theognis (lines 1249–52, 1335–36, 1337–40, 1351–52):

You're like a horse, boy; when you had your fill
Of barley, you came back to my stable, made
Desirous for cool springs, fine fields, my skill
As chariot driver, and my shady glade.

Happy the man who, going home, can play
With a pretty boy, sleeping with him all day.

No longer do I love a boy. I've shed
Sore troubles, painful toil I've gladly fled,
From fair-crowned Aphrodite's lust set free,
And your charm, boy, is nothing now to me.

Boy, don't revel. Take an old man's advice:
Carousing by a young man isn't nice.

The poems of Theognis, as well as the *skolia* and lyric poems sung or recited at a symposium, provided the context for much of the love epigrams of the Hellenistic poets. The themes and motifs of wine and love, of the fire of passion and pain of disappointment, are employed in almost endless variety in the epigrams. We can see this already in Asclepiades, who may have been the first of the Hellenistic poets to write such poems. Here is his epigram about an unhappy lover (GP 18, *AP* 12.135):

> Wine is the test of love. What he denied,
> The many toasts we made have verified,
> As weeping, nodding low, he hid his face,
> And his garland, tightly bound, slipped out of place.

The relationship of the poem to a symposium is made explicit by the "many toasts" and the "garland, tightly bound." So close is this connection in the early love epigrams of the third century that some have suggested that these poems were initially written for the purpose of recitation at dinner parties, or were even composed at a symposium extemporaneously. Cicero tells us that the Greek poets Archias and Antipater of Sidon could both compose epigrams *ex tempore,* and many others may also have had this ability. We should perhaps imagine groups of poets in Alexandria and elsewhere, reclining on couches and competing with one another to recite the cleverest poem; but since there is no actual evidence that the poets of the third century really did this, we may also wish to think of them in the quiet of their studies writing for later recitation and publication. These two possibilities are, of course, not mutually exclusive. And even if the poets themselves did not recite their love poems at dinner, it is difficult to believe that others would not have done so when the myrtle branch was passed their way, once these poems had found their way to booksellers.

Though the poets may not have competed face-to-face, they certainly were well aware of one another's verses and often wrote poems of a similar nature, turning the epigram of one poet into something different by a procedure that has come to be known by the Latin name *variatio.* The structure of the first poem could be altered or even inverted, the circumstances of the theme made more general or more particular, the poem made longer with the addition of new detail and a more focused, "pointed" ending, or shortened and given a different emphasis. The relationship to the earlier poem would nevertheless be made clear—similar words would be used at the beginning or end, or the same proper name mentioned somewhere in the poem, or a particular expression or situation repeated.

Here, for example, is a poem by Callimachus based on Asclepiades' poem cited above, again about a young man at a symposium suffering from disappointed love (GP 13, *AP* 12.134):

> The guest kept his wound secret. Did you see?
> The breath came from his chest so painfully;
> By the third toast, the roses had all shed
> Their petals to the floor down from his head.
> His goose is cooked, and this is no surmise:
> A thief, I know another thief's disguise.

Although Callimachus uses different words, the beginning of his poem introduces the same theme: the guest isn't talking, but it is obvious that something is up. From the weeping, the nodding low, the hidden face, and the slipping garland of Asclepiades, Callimachus picks up only the garland, whose dissolution he describes with greater vividness. He also includes two additional lines to provide a more tightly pointed ending. Other Hellenistic poets also took up this theme, each incorporating a different selection of structures and motifs.

One of the most popular kinds of love epigrams of Hellenistic poets was the *paraclausithyron*, a poem of a suitor before the closed door of his beloved. Greek men who had drunk a great deal of wine would roam about the town in a *komos* or revel, stopping before the door of an adolescent boy or a woman and asking to be admitted. If they weren't let in, they could turn violent and attempt to break the door down or set it afire.

In a more peaceful mood, they might recite a poem, like this one of Asclepiades (GP 13, *AP* 5.164):

> I call to witness only you:
> See, Night, what Pythiás can do,
> How she mistreats and tricks her paramour.
> Invited, not uncalled I came;
> May she, enduring just the same,
> Complain to you later, standing at my door.

As in many other such epigrams, the poet is unsuccessfully seeking entry and is grumbling about his ill-treatment. What is unusual in this poem is that the poet was actually invited to come (or at least *says* he was), a circumstance that makes the refusal of the woman even more galling and provides the occasion for the outburst of the last two lines.

Posidippus wrote this variation on the poem of Asclepiades (GP 4, *AP* 5.213):

> If Pythiás is busy, I won't stay;
> But if she sleeps alone, bring me inside.
> Give her this message: drunk, I made my way
> Through thieves, with reckless Eros as my guide.

Here, too, the poet is at the door of his beloved, and Posidippus uses the same proper name for the woman. By doing so, he directs us back to the poem of Asclepiades, indicating that we are to read one poem in relation to the other. In Asclepiades the door is closed and the poet cannot enter, but in Posidippus the door is open and the poet addresses not Night but a servant who appears in the doorway. There is no suggestion of a complaint, and certainly no bitterness. Instead, the poet is easygoing and complaisant, in contrast to the usual attitude of a lover in a poem of this sort, and his stance gives the epigram its amusing nonchalance—quite unlike the mood in Asclepiades.

This practice of *variatio,* of taking the themes and motifs of one poem and turning them into something related but different, was an integral part of the attitude of Hellenistic poets toward their tradition. For just as they adopted and then altered the conventions of inscriptions and earlier love poems that together provided the framework for their verse, so they took up and modified the epigrams of other poets. Because they were so acutely aware of their literary tradition, we too must attempt to learn as much as we can about it so that we can understand the context in which their poems were written. This context is not always clear, but I have attempted to provide something of what we do know in the notes to individual poems.

TEXTS OF EPIGRAMS

There seems little doubt that the Hellenistic poets, in a culture so conscious of the importance of collecting and preserving manuscripts, were careful to conserve their own poetry. For several, including Callimachus, we have evidence that books of their collected epigrams were published, and it is likely that nearly all the poets at one time or another put together a volume of their poems for distribution. For Posidippus we now have a sizable chunk of such a book, the recently discovered Milan papyrus, which might even have been compiled by the poet himself, though it is more likely to have been assembled by someone else after the poet's death. Except for Posidippus, however, all of these presumed editions of single poets remain lost, and we have only anthologies, or rather collations of transcriptions of anthologies.

Imagine that instead of the complete sonnets of Shakespeare, we had only the poems that Sir Arthur Quiller-Couch included in his *Oxford Book of English Verse*. Our notion of Shakespeare's art would be completely dependent on the taste of one Edwardian Englishman, who included many wonderful poems but omitted others we might wish he had also selected. Such is the case for a poet like Callimachus, for whom we have sixty-three complete (or nearly complete) epigrams, all but two from a massive collection of more than four thousand poems called the *Greek Anthology*. The poems of the *Greek Anthology* have come to us in turn from two manuscripts written in the Middle Ages—the *Palatine*

Anthology and the *Planudean Anthology*—which survived only by miraculous good fortune. The *Palatine* and *Planudean* anthologies contain many of the same poems, but each also has poems not found in the other. Both were apparently collated from the same anthology of Greek epigrams written somewhat earlier by Constantine Cephalas, a church official in the Byzantine palace.

Near the beginning of the tenth century CE, Cephalas assembled a very large number of Greek epigrams from a variety of sources, including earlier anthologies. Of the anthologies he used, the most important (at least for our purposes) were the *Garland* of Meleager (dating from about 100 BCE) and the *Garland* of Philip (40–50 CE). These books were called garlands because Meleager and later Philip referred to the poetry of the different poets as plants of different kinds, mostly flowers, which were intertwined in the anthology. The word *anthology* comes from this conceit: *anthos* means "flower," and *lego* is the verb to "pick up" or "gather."

From the two *Garlands,* Cephalas took the majority of the epigrams I have translated. He seems to have lifted most of these poems in large batches, since poems of the Hellenistic poets from Meleager's *Garland* (including those of Anyte, Leonidas, Asclepiades, Posidippus, Callimachus, and Meleager himself) often occur together in the *Greek Anthology* in stretches of sometimes more than a hundred poems; much the same is true for the work of later poets (including Philodemos) taken from Philip's *Garland.* The groupings from Meleager's *Garland* are arranged thematically, with those by more famous poets alternating with poems by lesser-known authors. Meleager often placed his own poems last in these clusters, as if to provide a kind of summary or cap to each of the poetic themes. This pattern is of some interest, since it shows that Meleager was conscious of the Hellenistic practice of *variatio* and wrote his own poems in direct response to the work of his predecessors (see the introduction to chapter 8).

The poems that Cephalas took from Philip's *Garland* seem to have been arranged according to a different principle, grouped alphabetically by the first letter of the first word of each poem. The sequence is not strictly alphabetical, since within each letter poems beginning for example with alpha were arranged thematically. Not all of the poems I have translated were taken from the two *Garlands;* in particular, Cephalas appears to have found the poems of Theocritus in a manuscript of pastoral poetry that also contained the *Idylls,* and he apparently took the poems of Lucillius from an anthology of Roman imperial poets that may have been assembled by Diogenian during the reign of Hadrian.

If Cephalas took most of the epigrams of Hellenistic poets directly from Meleager, then the poems that have survived were those Meleager chose for inclusion. Fortunately Meleager seems to have had fairly good taste, at least so far as we can judge. Our only evidence comes from the epigrams of Posidippus, since we can compare the poems in the *Greek Anthology* that Meleager selected, on a restricted number of themes (including love), with the epigrams in the Milan papyrus on a much broader range of subjects. Though many of the additional poems in the Milan papyrus are pleasant and nice to have, most would agree that the epigrams in Meleager's *Garland* are among Posidippus's best poems. Some scholars have even argued that the poems of the Milan papyrus cannot be by Posidippus, since for the most part they are not as good as the poems included by Meleager in his *Garland.* Although this is not a very convincing argument, it does suggest that Meleager was at least as good an anthologist as Quiller-Couch—perhaps even better.

Meleager probably worked from editions of collected poems, and he seems to have indicated the authorship of the epigrams at the top of or in the margin next to each poem. These attributions were then mostly appropriated by Cephalas and the collators of the *Palatine* and *Planudean* anthologies. But there are problems. Some poems lack attribution, or are listed as of uncertain authorship, or are ascribed to more than one poet. In choosing poems to translate, I have generally preferred those for which authorship is most clearly indicated, though even for these poems we can never be entirely certain that the attributions are correct.

The process of copying and recopying the poems, which was of course done entirely by hand, has left the text uncertain and even clearly defective in many places, and I have again attempted to choose the poems with the fewest difficulties. When the reading of the text is unclear, an editor can indicate all the variants and explain which ones seem the most likely. A translator after due consideration must decide on one reading from among the various possibilities and stick to it. In some cases I have explained my choices, but often I have not, since I think my preferences will be obvious to scholars and of little interest to the general reader.

Proper names have been transliterated according to the usual practice, but I make no claim of consistency. Well-known names have usually been left as most commonly given in English—so "Hercules" instead of "Herakles"; but I occasionally break this rule, preferring "Philodemos" to "Philodemus" to make clearer the joke in his poem III. Zeus is always "Zeus" and never "Jupiter," but I have sometimes used "Venus" for Aphrodite, "Cupid" for Eros, and "Love" for both.

I have indicated pronunciation of unfamiliar proper names in the poems because the general reader will need guidance, particularly in names of several syllables, but one should be aware that during the time the poems in this book were written, the pronunciation of Greek was changing from a tonal or pitch system somewhat like Chinese to one that is accentual, as in English or modern Greek. The solution I have adopted, while not entirely satisfactory, has at least the merit of letting the reader pronounce the name in the meter of the translation: I have placed an accent where the ancient Greeks would have put it on the nominative form of the name. I have not marked names likely to be familiar to the English reader; I have for example left "Anacreon" without indication, to be pronounced "Anácreon" as in *Merriam-Webster's,* even though in ancient Greek the tonal or stress mark was placed over the epsilon of the third syllable, Ἀνακρέων (Anacréon). Once again I have not been entirely consistent, and scholars who object in particular instances may wish to alter a poem's spelling or wording to suit their preference. They may do so with my blessing.

A NOTE ON TRANSLATIONS

This book is a short history of the Greek epigram as a genre, but it is not a history of a conventional sort. My aim has been to place the epigrams of ancient Greeks in context and to describe the work of the most important poets. I then let the poets speak for themselves by collecting representative poems in translation. Since there were nine Muses and nine poets in the canon of lyric verse in ancient Greece, I have chosen nine poets of epigrams as my exemplars. The choice was relatively easy and includes poets whom every scholar would place near the top of the list. For each author, I have translated about one-quarter to one-half of the total number of poems that have survived, probably a small fraction of the poet's total output. Taken together, these poems span a period of something like 350 years, during which the literary epigram rapidly emerged, underwent its remarkable flowering, and then altered to nearly the form it has now, two thousand years later.

All of the poems I have included (together with the inscriptions, *skolia,* fragments of Anacreon, selections from Theognis, and poems of other poets later in the volume) have been previously translated into prose, and many have been set in verse. I have not used those earlier versions but have provided my own translations, since it seemed essential in a book of this sort that everything come from the same hand. In that way, differences in theme and approach from one poet to another can more readily be attributed to differences between the poets rather than to differences between translators.

But I have another reason for doing new translations. What I love most about these poems is the clever way the poets adopted the brevity and succinctness they found originally in inscriptions, and then utilized this "epigrammatic" style even in poems about love. Most of the epigrams of the Greeks were not meant to be satirical and do not have a clever ending, but we can nevertheless recognize features of style and a manner of construction that permeate this genre, from the Greeks to Martial and up to the present day.

My goal therefore has been to make accurate translations of Greek epigrams that also convey something of this epigrammatic style. The importance of accuracy cannot be overemphasized. The better the translation, the more faithfully it retains the wording, word order, meaning, and structure of the original, and the greater the reader's ability to grasp what the poet was attempting to achieve. If a translation strays too far from the Greek, it becomes the poem of the translator rather than the poem of its author. Although this may be suitable in some contexts, it would be inappropriate in a book that attempts to use poems to illustrate the history of a genre.

Yet it isn't enough that a translation be accurate. It must also be a poem that resembles an epigram. All Greek (and Latin) epigrams were written in meter, but this meter was not based on the regular alternation of the stress of syllables as in English poetry. The ancient Greeks instead divided the line into feet according to the *quantity* of each of the syllables: that is, whether they were long (—) or short (◡). Syllables containing long vowels such as omega, eta, or diphthongs were nearly always long, whereas syllables containing vowels such as epsilon and omicron were short unless the vowels were followed by two consonants or a double consonant like a zeta or psi.

The most common meter used by the Greeks for their epigrams was the elegiac couplet, consisting of a line of dactylic hexameter (the meter of Homer and all other epic poetry) followed by a so-called "pentameter." The hexameter and pentameter lines are divided into feet according to the following scheme:

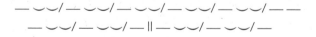

Each of the dactyls (— ◡ ◡) of the hexameter could be replaced by a spondee (— —), though rarely in the fifth foot. A *caesura,* or break between two words in the middle of a foot, was usually placed in the third foot of the hexameter. The pentameter consists of two symmetrical halves, each with two dactyls followed by a single long syllable; they are separated by a *diaeresis,* a break that occurs between two feet (indicated here by double vertical lines). Again, spondees could substitute for dactyls, but only in the first half of the line.

We can get something of the feel of how an elegiac couplet works by replacing the long syllables of the Greek with stressed syllables in English, and by filling the hexameter and pentameter lines with dactyls and spondees just as in our own verse. Here is an example:

$$— \cup\cup / — \cup\cup / — \cup\cup / — \cup\cup / — \cup\cup / — —$$

Hillary versus Barack: two exceptional candidates struggled.

$$— \cup\cup / — — / — \,\|\, — \cup\cup / — \cup\cup / —$$

After the fight was done, then we were left with just one.

Greeks often arranged the couplet so that the sense and wording of the hexameter contrasted in some way with that in the pentameter. I have attempted to imitate this feature by having the "two candidates" in the first line become "one" in the second. In the pentameter, the metrical division of the line into two halves encouraged the division of sense, often accentuated by temporal contrast or by parallel phrasing or antithesis. The ends of the two halves of the pentameter also occasionally rhymed, as do "done" and "one" in my couplet. A Greek poem with such a rhyme appears later in the chapter, but rhyme was used only occasionally and was rarely part of a regular scheme. Scholars inclined to say that Greek epigrams never had anything like a rhyme scheme should look at Lucillius *AP* 11.131, though that poem is admittedly an exception.

One approach to translating Greek epigrams might thus be to transform them into elegiac couplets, like the one about Secretary Clinton and President Obama. The difficulty, however, is that the elegiac couplet is a Greek (and Latin) meter, not an English meter, and the expectation produced in the mind of a Greek poet or reader by the regular succession of hexameters and pentameters after years of reading and writing this verse is impossible to reproduce in us. An English poem written in elegiac couplets tends to fall flat and bears little resemblance to our conception of an epigram.

English epigrams have their own meter, traditionally iambic pentameter in a regular rhyme scheme of pairs of lines (aa bb cc) called heroic couplets. Almost all the epigrams of Ben Jonson and John Donne were written in this way, and most later poets followed the same pattern. Here is Donne's epigram on a licentious person growing old:

> Thy sins and hairs may no man equal call;
> For, as thy sins increase, thy hairs do fall.

More than three hundred years later, J. V. Cunningham wrote an epigram about an inexperienced young man and a free-spirited woman:

> Young Sensitive one summer on the Cape
> Met a Miss Splash. She led him to a rape
> Through all the jagged colors of her mood.
> It was like sleeping with an abstract nude.

English poets wrote epigrams like this for the same reason that the Greeks wrote them in elegiac couplets. The meter (and rhyme) produce an expectation in the reader that helps convey the meaning of the poem; in a satirical epigram, they are an essential part of the "point" at the end.

Hence a second approach might be to convert the elegiac couplets of the Greeks into heroic couplets in English, as was done for three of the poems of Asclepiades, Callimachus, and Posidippus that I cited earlier in the section on love epigram. Many previous translations of Greek epigrams have relied on this method. But there is a problem: the lines of an elegiac couplet are longer than those of an heroic couplet. A Greek or Latin hexameter can contain as many as seventeen syllables and the "pentameter" as many as fourteen, whereas an English iambic pentameter line usually contains only ten and at most eleven or twelve syllables. Furthermore, Greek is an inflected language, and a single adjective must sometimes be translated by an entire phrase of English. As a result, it often takes more than two lines of English verse to render two lines of Greek, and in many poems I found it impossible to translate an elegiac couplet into an heroic couplet. Since both Greek and English poets have occasionally used alternative meters for epigrams, I decided that I could do this too, so long as the result still conveys something of the succinctness and verve of the epigrammatic style.

My method is best illustrated by example. The three I give are all poems that, for one reason or another, I couldn't translate directly into heroic couplets, and that forced me to make compromises to fit the Greek into a regular English metrical and rhyme scheme. They should give some feeling for the degree of accommodation required to do the translations, particularly in poems that posed difficulties.

My first example is a *paraclausithyron* of Asclepiades (GP 13, *AP* 5.164), a poem I described earlier in the chapter. I give the Greek here (and only in this part of the book) to convey a sense of the original:

νύξ, σὲ γάρ, οὐκ ἄλλην, μαρτύρομαι, οἷά μ' ὑβρίζει
    Πυθιὰς ἡ Νικοῦς οὖσα φιλεξαπάτις.
κληθείς, οὐκ ἄκλητος, ἐλήλυθα· ταῦτα παθοῦσα
    σοὶ μέμψαιτ' ἔτ' ἐμοῖς στᾶσα παρὰ προθύροις.

Notice the rhyme at the ends of the two halves of the pentameter in line 4 between ἐμοῖς (*emois*) and προθύροις (*prothyrois*):

— — / — ⏑⏑/ — ‖ — ⏑⏑/ — ⏑⏑/ —
σοὶ μέμψαιτ' ἔτ' ἐμοῖς στᾶσα παρὰ προθύροις
(*soi mempsait' et' em<u>ois</u> ‖ stasa para prothyr<u>ois</u>*)

The literal translation of the poem in prose is:

Night—for you, no other, do I call to witness how Niko's Pythias, loving to deceive, mistreats me. Invited, not uninvited, have I come; suffering the same, may she complain to you later, standing at my door.

And here is my verse translation (Asclepiades XI), which I gave earlier in the chapter but repeat here for convenience:

> I call to witness only you:
> See, Night, what Pythiás can do,
> How she mistreats and tricks her paramour.
> Invited, not uncalled I came;
> May she, enduring just the same,
> Complain to you later, standing at my door.

For this poem the four lines of Greek required six of English but not six lines of iambic pentameter, so I used pentameters for lines 3 and 6 and gave the rest as tetrameters. I decided to move the vocative νύξ, "Night," from the very beginning of the poem to the second line, and to put σὲ, "you," at the end of the first line. I added the word "do," which is not in the Greek, for clarity and for the rhyme with "you." I also translated φιλεξαπάτις, "loving to deceive," as a verb ("trick") instead of as an adjective, and I replaced the "me" of the poem with "her paramour" to produce the rhyme at the end with "door."

Asclepiades describes Pythias as Πυθιὰς ἡ Νικοῦς, Niko's Pythias. Proper names often create problems, and I have sometimes left them out if they were difficult to fit into the structure of the poem and seemed to me to serve no specific purpose. The name Pythias of course could not be left out, since, as we previously saw, this same name also shows up in an epigram of Posidippus and serves as a point of reference between the two poems. But because we are never told who Niko is or what relation she bears to Pythias or to the rest of the poem, I didn't include her. Apart from these alterations, my translation follows the original reasonably closely. In particular, my "invited, not uncalled I came" reproduces the word order of κληθείς, οὐκ ἄκλητος, ἐλήλυθα, and my translation of the last sentence follows the Greek nearly word for word.

My next example is also a *paraclausithyron,* but this time from Callimachus (GP 8, *AP* 12.118, Pf 42):

εἰ μὲν ἑκών, Ἀρχῖν᾽, ἐπεκώμασα μυρία μέμφου,
　　εἰ δ᾽ ἄκων ἥκω τὴν προπέτειαν ἔα.
ἄκρητος καὶ ἔρως μ᾽ ἠνάγκασαν, ὧν ὁ μὲν αὐτῶν
　　εἷλκεν, ὁ δ᾽ οὐκ εἴα τὴν προπέτειαν ἐᾶν·
ἐλθὼν δ᾽ οὐκ ἐβόησα τίς ἢ τίνος ἀλλ᾽ ἐφίλησα
　　τὴν φλιήν. εἰ τοῦτ᾽ ἐστ᾽ ἀδίκημ᾽ ἀδικέω.

Here is a literal translation of the poem:

If willingly, Archinus, I have caroused, then blame me at length (or "ten thousand times"), but if unwillingly I have come, then let my rashness go. Undiluted wine and Eros compelled me, of which the one dragged me along, and the other didn't allow me to forgo my rashness. Having come I did not call out who [I was] or whose (i.e., my patronymic), but I kissed the doorpost. If that is a sin then I have sinned.

And here is my verse translation (Callimachus XXV):

If I caroused, Archínos, under no
　　Constraint, then my behavior blame
　　Ten thousand times, but if I came
Unwillingly, then let my rashness go.

For undiluted wine and Eros placed
　　Me in their thrall, the one conveyed
　　Me onward, and the other made
Me powerless to put aside my haste.

I've come but do not ask to be admitted;
　　Giving no name, I placed a kiss
　　Upon the doorpost, and if this
Is wrong, then wrong is what I have committed.

The six lines of Callimachus's epigram are so wonderfully condensed that my translation required twelve lines of English, which I divided into stanzas to make the poem easier to read. Each stanza translates an elegiac couplet and follows the structure and word order of Callimachus's poem as closely as possible. I had to make some choices about word usage. For example, I translated the word μυρία as "ten thousand times," since μύριοι is literally the number "ten thousand." This word can however also mean "an indefinitely large number," but I have tried in many instances to preserve literal meaning, since it conveys something of the character of the Greek. The beginning of the last couplet says in Greek "having come, I did not call out who or whose (my name or the name of my father)." Now, it would have been evident to a contemporary of Callimachus that if the poet standing at the door had called out his name and patronymic, he would have been asking to be admitted. I decided this wouldn't be clear to a modern reader, so I added "admitted." But because it was nevertheless important to make clear that the poet did not give his name, I say that too. It didn't seem necessary to add the patronymic, since we normally do not provide it when we "give our name" in English.

My last example is from Posidippus (GP 20, AB 15) and is an epigram about a gemstone said to be from the head of a snake.

οὐ ποταμὸς κελάδων ἐπὶ χείλεσιν ἀλλὰ δράκοντος
　　εἶχέ ποτ᾽ εὐπώγων τόνδε λίθον κεφαλή
πυκνὰ φαληριόωντα· τὸ δὲ γλυφὲν ἅρμα κατ᾽ αὐτοῦ
　　τοῦθ᾽ ὑπὸ Λυγκείου βλέμματος ἐγλύφετο
ψεύδεϊ χειρὸς ὅμοιον· ἀποπλασθὲν γὰρ ὁρᾶται
　　ἅρμα, κατὰ πλάτεος δ᾽ οὐκ ἂν ἴδοις προβόλους·
ἦ καὶ θαῦμα πέλει μόχθου μέγα, πῶς ὁ λιθουργὸς
　　τὰς ἀτενιζούσας οὐκ ἐμόγησε κόρας.

My literal translation is similar to those of Nisetich and of Austin and Bastianini:

> It was not a river rumbling in its banks, but the bearded head of a snake that once held this gem, thickly streaked with white. The chariot engraved on it was engraved by Lynkeian eyesight, like the mark on a fingernail; for the chariot is seen to be incised, but on the surface you would not notice protrusions. Wherefore there is such great amazement at the work, how the gem engraver did not overwork his eyesight as he gazed intently.

And here is my verse translation (Posidippus XIX):

No river rumbling in its banks, instead
    A bearded snake head
Once bore this gem with ample streaks of white.
    Lýnkeian eyesight
Engraved on it a chariot, as fine
    As a mark or line
On a fingernail, incised, with no part raised.
    You would be amazed
A jeweler could carve this, without impairing
    His eyes from staring.

The poem in Greek is in elegiac couplets and is eight lines long. As a general rule, the longer the poem, the easier it is to find a suitable translation in English in heroic couplets, since more words afford a greater opportunity for rhyming. With this poem, however, I could not find an appropriate translation in that meter. As I was struggling with heroic couplets, the first four lines suddenly came to me in a different meter consisting of one line of iambic pentameter alternating with one syllabic line of five syllables. It would be inaccurate to say that I chose this meter; it chose me. Since Hellenistic poets occasionally used couplets of an unconventional composition, I decided to stick with these first four lines, at least provisionally. The difficulty then became to fill in the rest of the poem.

I began by changing the sentence about Lynkeian eyesight from passive to active voice (as Nisetich also does). Lynkeus was one of the crew of the *Argo,* the ship that sailed in search of the golden fleece, and he was proverbial for his keen sight. I then greatly condensed "for the chariot is seen to be incised, but on the surface you would not notice protrusions" to simply "incised, with no part raised." I also changed the wording of the last sentence, again condensing a bit and simplifying. The result is "to say almost the same thing," as Umberto Eco put it in *Dire quasi la stessa cosa,* his perceptive book about translation. I have attempted to preserve as much of the wording of the verse as I could, but in a medium in English that reproduces some of the feeling of the poem as an epigram.

These examples are representative of the difficulties I encountered and the approach I used to solve them. I have made every attempt to produce translations as faithful to the original as possible, but I made some compromises to produce a poem with meter and rhyme. I have occasionally left out a name or patronymic or vocative or other word or phrase that didn't seem to me essential, or added a word or phrase to make the meaning clearer. In some poems I have condensed and simplified; in others, I have expanded the poem by saying the same thing more than once, either to explain a word with more than one meaning or to fill in the structure of the poem. I have attempted to make these changes as conservatively as I could, with careful attention to the meaning of the Greek.

Traduttore, traditore; there is no perfect translation. Readers wishing to compare my versions with those of other translators may want to consult the many volumes listed under "Texts of Poems" in the bibliography at the back of the book. I hope my own renditions give some feeling for these charming, amusing, and occasionally moving poems, which are not as well known as they should be, and which have played such an important role in the history of Western literature.

CHAPTER TWO

Anyte

The most famous woman poet of ancient Greece was of course Sappho, whose work has come down to us mostly as fragments cited by other authors or in papyri rescued from the sands of Egypt. We have only two, perhaps three of her poems in their entirety. From Anyte, on the other hand, we have at least twenty, which may never reach the summit of the greatest of Sappho's verses but nevertheless deserve more attention than they have received. Anyte's lovely and affecting epigrams about young women and animals are among the most enjoyable poems of Meleager's *Garland*. She is also important historically, since she was among the first to extend the genre of epigram beyond the customary categories of epitaphs and dedications.

Of Anyte's life we know practically nothing. She is said to have come from Tegea in Arcadia, in a mountainous area in the south of mainland Greece in the middle of the Peloponnesian Peninsula. Her birth date is uncertain but is likely to have been near 340–320 BCE, since she was apparently active at the very beginning of the third century BCE. One of the few stories we have about her is given by Pausanias in his *Description of Greece*. The tale goes that a rich man named Phalysius in the city of Naupactus had an eye disease. When he was nearly blind, Asclepius, the Greek god of medicine, appeared to Anyte in a dream and gave her a sealed tablet, which she was instructed to take to Phalysius. When she arrived in Naupactus, she told Phalysius to take off the seal and read what was written. When Phalysius looked at the tablet, he realized that he had recovered his sight and did as he was instructed: he gave Anyte two thousand staters of gold, which would have made her quite a wealthy woman.

Anyte's influence on Greek epigram was immense. She wrote epitaphs and dedications, in most cases not as actual inscriptions but for recitation and publication. She was among the first of the Greek poets to write epitaphs for dead animals, which subsequently became a major theme of third-century poetry. She was also apparently among the first to write poems whose themes lay outside the traditional scope of epigrams and were epideictic—that is, written to display the talents of the poet on almost any subject. They included poems we now call ecphrastic, which describe a work of art such as a piece of sculpture or a painting. Since we probably have only a fraction of her output, we cannot know how far she took the epigram outside its traditional boundaries, but the poems of the later poet Posidippus make clear that the range subsequently became very large, and Anyte likely played an important role in this development.

There is an elegance and sensitivity to her writing that is greater than in many of the other Hellenistic poets. Her epitaphs on young women (I–IV) are poignant expressions of grief of the parents and friends of the dead girls. The voice of these poems seems to be that of the poet, as if

Anyte had known each of these girls personally. The epitaphs and con-
solation poems for dead animals (VI–X) are varied in character, but
several are remarkable for their sympathy to pets and the world of nature.
We can scarcely doubt that the Greeks were fond of animals; we need
only remember the portrayal in book 17 of the *Odyssey* of the dog Argos,
who, though near death, dropped his ears and wagged his tail at the
sound of his master's voice. Anyte brought this appreciation to a higher
level, anticipating the famous poem of Catullus on the death of Lesbia's
sparrow.

Her poems on rural themes (XI–XV) were also influential. These
epigrams highlight the lives of simple people living in the mountainous
countryside, perhaps of Arcadia. Epigrams featuring shepherds and
goats, often with nymphs and the god Pan, were also written by other
Greek poets (see Leonidas XX–XXIII, XXV–XXVI; Theocritus X),
and Arcadian shepherds later appear in Virgil's *Eclogues* and in the art
and literature of Europe during the Renaissance, in works by Poussin
and Sidney among many others. Although the present state of our
knowledge does not let us trace the patterns of influence in any detail, it
is likely that Anyte's epigrams were an important stimulus to the emer-
gence of the pastoral tradition.

The poems of this original poet were significant in another respect.
As one of the earliest of the third-century poets to make people of hum-
ble origin the subject of her poems, she helped initiate a motif that recurs
in much of subsequent Greek poetry. The life not just of shepherds but
also of carpenters, housewives, and fishermen became one of the most
important themes of poets such as Leonidas of Tarentum and Theocritus.
The popularity of this poetry reflects a fascination of the Hellenistic age,
displayed not only in literature but in all of the arts, with whatever
seemed novel or unusual to city-dwelling Greeks. We may wish to call
this realism, but the "reality" these poems present is more a product of
the imagination of the poets than a reflection of the actual life of shep-
herds and farmers in the Greek countryside.

Anyte used the structure and conventional themes of the epigram to

write a poetry strikingly different from earlier epitaphs and dedications
and also unlike the lyric poetry of Sappho and the other archaic Greek
poets. Her portrait of a dolphin (epigram VII) resembles nothing else in
earlier Greek poetry. There is a poignant contrast between the playful
and spirited swimming in the first half of the poem and the stillness of
the dead body at the end. Whether this epigram was intended to accom-
pany a painting or written just to describe a sadness the poet had experi-
enced, we cannot help but share her feeling for the dolphin and her sen-
sitivity to the harshness of its fate. There can be no better poet to begin
our survey of this remarkable poetry.

I

Kleína called out over this tomb and cried
    When doom too early came,
Often mourning her cherished child who died,
    Calling the soul by name
Of Philainís, who unwed had to go
Beyond the river Acheron's pale flow.

II

In place of wedding songs and bridal room,
Your mother set upon this marble tomb
A maiden with your grace and form instead,
So, Thérsis, we could greet you though you're dead.

III

When Erató her two arms cast
Around her father, she these last
Words spoke, as tears began to pour:
"Oh father, see, I am no more,
Across my eyes black death has spread
And covers me, already dead."

IV

I mourn this girl, to whose house bridegrooms came,
So many stirred to longing from her fame
Of beauty and good sense, but out of reach
Pernicious fortune tossed the hopes of each.

V

This man called Manes was a slave, when he
  Was living once; but dead,
  As powerful instead
As Darius the Great he now can be.

VI

Oh Lokris, by dense-rooted brush you died,
Yap-loving puppy with the fleetest stride.
A snake with neck of many colors put
Such brutal venom in your nimble foot.

VII

No longer sporting in the waves by ships
  Shall I break out, and throw
  My neck up from below,
Nor round the rowlocks puff my pretty lips

And snort, proud of my figurehead, and breach.
  The dark swell of the sea
  To land delivered me,
And now I lie beside this slender beach.

VIII

This marker Dámis put, when Ares slew
His brave steed; from the chest, dark blood boiled through
The thick, tough hide, and then began to pour,
Drenching the clods of earth with doleful gore.

IX

Together in a tomb Myró had made,
A locust, nightingale of fields, was laid
With a cicada, dweller of the trees;
    And as she built the bier,
    She shed a maiden's tear,
That willful Hades would both playthings seize.

X

No longer wakening, close wings outspread,
Will you at daybreak rouse me from my bed;
A brigand, secretly approaching, smote
You sleeping, with a quick claw to the throat.

XI

To rough-haired Pan and to the nymphs of a cave,
Beneath this peak the shepherd Theúdotos gave
This gift, because with water, honey-sweet,
    They reached their hands out
And freshened him, exhausted by the heat,
    During a summer drought.

XII

Oh rustic Pan by lonely thicket, say
Why, sitting, you sweet-sounding reed-pipe play?
"So heifers down this dewy mountain pass
May pasture, plucking thick-leaved tips of grass."

XIII

The youths who put the red reins, billy goat,
And muzzle round your shaggy nose and throat,
 Are training you to race
 Like horses, in the space
Round the god's temple, so that he can see
How they amuse themselves with childlike glee.

XIV

Sit down beneath these lovely leaves of bay,
Take sweet drink from the spring, that you may ease
Your dear limbs, gasping from a summer's day
Of labor, beaten by a zephyr's breeze.

XV

Friend, rest your weary limbs beneath this peak—
See how the sweet breeze makes the green leaves speak—
And drink from this cold spring, in summer heat
A welcome resting-place for tired feet.

EXPLANATORY NOTES

I (GP 5, AP 7.486)

All of the first four epigrams that I have selected were written for young
women who died too soon and before their time. Several actual epitaphs
for unmarried girls survive from the fourth century, written perhaps not
long before Anyte wrote this poem. It is sometimes said that Anyte's epi-
taph is itself an inscription for a tomb, but an inscription is unlikely to
describe mourning that could have taken place only after the tomb was
erected. The voice of the poem belongs neither to the girl nor her mother
but to an anonymous third person, perhaps the poet. The river Acheron

is the river of the underworld in Greek mythology over which Charon had to ferry the souls of the dead. The water of the Acheron in the last line is *chloros,* a color that in Greek can mean green (as in chlorophyll) but also yellow, and it is often associated in love poetry with youth. Here, however, the word probably means "pallid" or "pale," in Homer the color of fear.

II (GP 8, AP 7.649)

Another poem for an unwed girl, describing a tomb having on its top a statue of the deceased. It resembles many actual inscriptions for young women dating from the fourth century (see chapter 1).

III (GP 7, AP 7.646)

This touching poem, though not an epitaph, might have accompanied a relief for a tomb showing the father and daughter, but it might simply be book poetry. We can assume that Erato died before her marriage, since it is her father who is at her bedside rather than a husband or children. The language of the Greek is simple, as I have tried to convey in the translation, but many of the words and word forms have an epic or tragic overtone.

IV (GP 6, AP 7.490)

The voice of the epigram is again that of an anonymous mourner. It is difficult to read this poem and not think of epic models—of Helen, whose suitors included many of the great heroes of the *Iliad,* or of Penelope, wife of Ulysses. The verb Anyte uses in the last line (*kylindo*) means to "toss" or "roll along" and is often used by Homer of the waves of the sea. It is used here metaphorically of fortune, which can resemble a wave tossing flotsam to one side.

V (GP 24, AP 7.538)

This famous poem is attributed to Anyte in the *Palatine Anthology* but appears in the *Planudean* without attribution. This element of uncertainty, together with the philosophical tone of the poem, unlike anything else in Anyte's verse, has caused some scholars to doubt whether she wrote it. It is unlikely to be an actual inscription, since slaves were rarely given tombs with markers. Darius the Great was king of Persia; it was his army that the Greeks defeated at Marathon in 490 BCE. Darius would have been dead long before this poem was written. The poem reverses the common notion that death brings even the greatest king down to the level of his lowest subject.

VI (GP 10)

The next five poems I have chosen are among those Anyte wrote for dead animals. The name of the puppy, Lokris, means "Locrian," and Locrian dogs are mentioned in Xenophon as especially good for hunting boar. The puppy (as in epitaphs I–IV) is female—the gender is clear in the Greek though not indicated in the translation. The extensive use of compound adjectives in this poem and elsewhere in Anyte is Homeric (compare the familiar "wine-dark" sea). The viper is *poikilodeiros:* that is, it has a neck of many colors, from *poikilos,* meaning "variegated," and *deire,* meaning "neck."

VII (GP 12, AP 7.215)

A marine animal is tossed up onto the shore. The name of the animal is not given in the poem, but the description is clearly that of a dolphin. We see again in this poem a sympathy for an animal and for nature that is rare before the Hellenistic era, perhaps before Anyte herself. The interpretation of the middle section of the poem is disputed. I have translated it to give the dolphin puffing out its lips near the figurehead, since I think this is an affecting reading perfectly consistent with the Greek. Some scholars, however, would interpret the word *cheilos* or "lip" to refer to the stem or cutwater of the ship, effectively removing the dolphin's lips from the poem. I have translated Anyte's word *skalmos* as "rowlocks," but its literal translation is "thole" or "thole pin." The thole pin, probably made of hardwood, was placed in the oar port, and the oar (held in place by a strap) was fitted to one side of the thole and pivoted against it.

VIII (GP 9, AP 7.208)

This is the only poem of Anyte about a dead animal that purports to be an actual inscription. It reads very much like a memorial, not for a warrior fallen in battle but rather for his horse. Ares is the Greek god of war, and to say that "Ares slew" the horse is simply to say that the horse died in battle. This is a poem of remarkable violence, different in character from the rest of the animal poems.

IX (GP 20, AP 7.190)

Among the first of many epigrams written by Greek poets for dead insects. For one of the insects Anyte uses the Greek word *akris,* which may be either a locust (grasshopper) or a cricket. I have translated it "locust," since Leonidas X was probably written in imitation of Anyte's poem, and Leonidas describes the *akris* as "walking on thorns," which far better suits a locust or grasshopper than a cricket (crickets are ground dwelling). Locusts and cicadas, mentioned in Greek poetry as early as Homer and Hesiod, were prized for their singing. To an American or northern European, the continual noise made by male cicadas may seem irritating, but the ancient Greeks thought the sound charming. There are many references in Greek epigrams to the keeping of insects as pets, much as the Chinese keep crickets in small cages to enjoy their pleasant chirping. Some have identified the Myro of the poem with Moero, another woman poet, who may have been a contemporary of Anyte. The compound adjective Anyte uses to describe the cicada—*dryokoites,* or "dweller of the trees"—is found nowhere else in Greek; she may have made it up.

X (GP 11, AP 7.202)

A rooster is killed by a predator such as a weasel, the "brigand" of the poem. There is some irony that the cock, who usually woke the poet at daybreak, has itself been caught napping.

XI (GP 3, APl 291)

This is a dedication, perhaps intended for an inscription next to a spring. It is remarkable, however, in being offered not by a wealthy maiden or athletic victor to one of the major deities but by a shepherd to Pan and the nymphs. If Anyte did indeed come from Arcadia, the choice of Pan is fitting, since this shepherd god was often associated by the Greeks with that part of the Peloponnese. The nature of the gift left at the spring isn't specified in the poem, but country shrines were often adorned with statues or small paintings and reliefs (as seen even now at wayside shrines in the Italian countryside).

XII (GP 19, APl 231)

Another poem on a rural theme, again including Pan. It is, however, neither an epitaph nor a dedication but a novel kind of epigram that Anyte may have been among the first to write. It may have accompanied a work of art; surviving inscriptions for wall paintings in Pompeii have taught us that poems could accompany paintings. The form of the poem is question and answer, divided evenly between two elegiac couplets (in my translation, two heroic couplets). Reported speech is very rare in surviving inscriptions but becomes more common in the literary epigrams of the third-century poets; see, for example, Leonidas XII and XXVI, Posidippus XIV, and Callimachus VI, VII, and XVIII.

XIII *(GP 13, AP 6.312)*

Like the previous poem, this delightful vignette of children playing with a billy goat may have been intended to accompany a painting or sculpture, or it may have been written merely to express the poet's pleasure at the joy of happy boys and girls. Poems about children are rare in Greek literature. The goat in the poem continues the rural theme. The text at the end is uncertain; I have adopted the reading of Gow and Page.

XIV and XV *(GP 16, AP 9.313 and GP 18, APl 228)*

The final two poems I have selected take us back to the country spring in summer heat of poem XI. In *Poetic Garlands,* Kathryn Gutzwiller has suggested that these two poems are programmatic and that one or both may have been placed at the beginning of a book of Anyte's verse. In the first of the poems, the reader is invited to sit down under the lovely leaves of a bay (or laurel) tree, the tree sacred to Apollo, the god of poetry. The "spring" in the poem may be the fount of song, from which we take "sweet drink" by reading the poems. The drink is cold and refreshing because the poems are novel in style and theme. The second poem has a similar subject, beginning (as do many grave inscriptions) with an address to the passerby. A zephyr is a west wind, and the phrase "beaten by a zephyr's breeze" in XIV is taken from book 11 of the *Iliad,* where Hector, for the moment routing the Greeks, is compared to a zephyr striking the clouds and driving them away. Anyte uses the same word for "strike" or "beat" but puts it in the passive voice instead of the active. To have one's "dear limbs" struck by the gentle west wind on a hot day would be refreshing and would add to the attraction of the spring.

CHAPTER THREE

Leonidas of Tarentum

Meleager preserved more epigrams of Leonidas of Tarentum in his *Garland* than of any poet apart from Meleager himself. Leonidas may have been a special favorite of the anthologist or particularly prolific, but the large number of his poems must surely also reflect his immense reputation in antiquity. Leonidas's epigrams were the most frequently imitated of any of the Hellenistic poets; they were cited by Cicero, translated by Propertius, and inscribed on the walls of houses in Pompeii. He was famous for his portraits of simple working people, of weavers and carpenters and fishermen, in poems that have a touching charm and sympathy. Although the subjects of the poems are often humble and from the lower classes, the poetry itself is erudite, with many novel word forms and complex syntax. It could have been written only by a man of great culture with a highly educated audience in mind.

Nearly everything we know about the life of Leonidas must be inferred from his poems. He came from Tarentum, which at the beginning of the third century was a bustling Greek settlement and seaport in the south of Italy (now Taranto). The many learned allusions and literary expressions scattered throughout his poetry indicate that he had received an extensive education, which would have been possible only if he had been born into privilege. He speaks with some bitterness of the life of a wanderer (see for example XXVII), and this and other evidence suggests that he left Tarentum, probably under duress; since there are no references in his poems to the Romans, it is probably a safe assumption that he left before Tarentum fell to the Roman army in 272 BCE. He says he was poor (XIV, XXVII, and XXVIII), perhaps having run out of money after a long absence from home; but we should not necessarily take him at his word, since we have no way now of separating reality from poetic stance. The emphasis in his poetry on the common man and the presence of rural themes in several epigrams indicate that Leonidas was familiar with the poetry of Anyte. His epigram XX in particular is modeled on her XI (and his X on her IX). It is reasonable guess, then, that Leonidas was born after Anyte, but we cannot exclude the possibility that the two poets were near contemporaries. We do not know when Leonidas died, but he may have lived to an old age, since he refers to himself as old in one of his poems (XXVIII). What Leonidas meant by "old" is difficult to tell; Horace thought himself old (and indeed may have been) in his early fifties.

Like Anyte, Leonidas wrote poems mostly in the form of epitaphs and dedications, only a small fraction of which could conceivably have been written to be engraved on stone. Also like Anyte, he wrote about common people and rural subjects in poems often addressed to gods of the forest and field instead of to the usual pantheon of Greek mythology, but his extant poetry encompasses a wider range of subjects than does hers. Many of his epitaphs are portraits in miniature, sometimes bizarre and improbable, often good-natured and compassionate with evident feeling for his subjects. He used the form of a dedication to assemble long lists of tools—for example, of a carpenter (XVI) or a fisherman (XVII); in so doing, he gave a glimpse into the lives of workmen of his time. A dedication in his hands could also be satire (XVIII) or a pretext for a story on a rural theme (XXI and XXII). He wrote epideictic or "display" poems on many different subjects and was among the first to compose invective epigrams like those later made famous by Lucillius and Martial, addressed to fictitious characters representing types rather than actual people. He was also among the first to write epigrams to Priapus, the god of fertility, and his epigram XXX and similar poems by later Greek writers had an enormous influence on Latin poetry.

Much of his work was influenced by Cynic philosophy, whose founder Diogenes wore the garb of a vagrant beggar and advocated extreme asceticism. It is Diogenes who is said to have traversed Athens holding a lighted lamp in daylight, looking for an honest man. Throughout the third century the Cynic, with his wallet and threadbare cloak and staff, was a familiar figure in the Greek world. The Cynics placed special emphasis on self-sufficiency: a man should be content with his lot and not fear death, but (according to the Cynic Bion) leave his body as he would "leave a house when the landlord, failing to get the rent, takes away the door or the slating."

Many of Leonidas's poems show a Cynic influence (of those I have translated, see especially XI, XII, XXVII, and XXVIII). The Cynics were noted for a kind of writing called *spoudaiogeloion* (literally, "serious comedy"), consisting of satirical poems or folktales that were funny but with a somber, usually ethical theme. This genre may have been the inspiration for poems like VI and XXVI. There are, however, numerous indications in the surviving work that Leonidas was not himself a faithful adherent to the Cynic creed (see for example VII and note). A true Cynic embraced a life of wandering and poverty, but these are just what

Leonidas says he fears and dislikes. If he was frugal, he may been so by necessity rather than by choice.

Like Anyte, Leonidas was greatly influenced by Homer and incorporated many compound adjectives and archaic word forms into his poems. It is not uncommon to find in his poetry words present nowhere else in Greek literature, many of them perhaps invented for the occasion. He had an uncommon fondness for rhetorical organization, for antithesis, as well as for parallel structure, pointed repetition, and enumeration. In some poems he carried these features to extreme lengths, and his style can seem overburdened and plodding. Unfortunately, these weaker poems are the ones that were most often imitated by later poets, but we should be careful not to judge Leonidas too harshly on this account. He is certainly not the only poet who has been more admired for his faults than his virtues, and it is unfair to hold him responsible for the effluvia left in his wake. Like every poet, he should be judged from his best poems. By this standard, he was one of the most important authors of Greek epigram in the history of the genre, whose influence, for better *and* for worse, was widespread and pervasive.

I

Of wretched Alkiménes, my
    Good sir, me you may call
The little tomb, the small supply
    Of earth; if overall
With bramble and sharp thorn I lie
    Now hidden, even so
Of Alkiménes once was I
    The barrow long ago.

II

Whoever are you? By this highway road,
    Whose are these sad bones lying bare,
    In coffin half-exposed to air?
The wheel and wagon axle with their load

Rub smooth the mound and marker, passing through;
    Soon even ribs, poor man, will lie
    For carts to crush as they go by,
And no one will be there to cry for you.

III

Do not, when you go sailing overseas,
    In length or breadth of vessel trust;
One squall can master any ship. One breeze
    Smote Prómachos, the massed wave thrust
The sailors in its hollow. But his doom
    Was not all bad: in his own land
He had from relatives both rites and tomb,
    When rough seas left him on the strand.

IV

Fish pirate, seiner, thrice-old Theris, who
Lived from his lucky fishing traps, and knew
How better than a gull to swim and dip
Down into pools, not in a great-oared ship
A sailor whom Arcturus slew, no blast
Of storm his decades ended, but he passed
Away from old age in his hut, with no
Clear cause, out like a lamp. And even so,
No wife or children made this marker then,
But the guild of fellow-working fishermen.

V

Often she shook off evening and morning sleep,
The old woman Platthís, so she could keep
Poverty far distant; grizzled and grayed,
To distaff and to spindle, spinner's aide,
She sang until the dawn around the place
Of the long course of Athena, moving with grace,
Twirling in wrinkled hand on wrinkled knee
Enough thread for the loom; lovely was she,
At eighty years the Acheron perceiving,
Who, beautiful, was beautifully weaving.

VI

 Here Maronís, wine-lover, lies,
Mere ashes made of wine jars she drank up;
 And everyone can recognize
Above her tomb an Attic drinking cup.

 She does not mourn, below the earth,
The sons and husband now of her bereft,
 To whom she gave a life of dearth,
But this: that in the cup there's nothing left.

VII

Oh you this grave of temperate
 Eúboulos who pass by,
Let's drink! The harbor's Hades that
 All go to when we die.

VIII

Shore-fisher Parmis, whom none could surpass,
Kallígnotos's son, a spearer of wrasse
And furious perch that snatches up the bait,
And fish that in hollow caves and deep rocks wait,
Once took his first catch from the sea and tried
To bite down on his deadly prey, and died.
For from his hand it, slimy, darted free
And wriggled down his narrow throat, and he
Rolled over, letting out his final breath,
And by his pole, fishhooks, and lines met death,
So filling up the fateful threads of doom.
The fisher Fischer made for him this tomb.

IX

I'm buried on the land and in the sea.
The Fates did this amazing thing to me,
To Thársys, son of Charmídes. For once I
Dove to a heavy anchor, come to lie
Fast in the seabed; going down below
Ionian swell, I saved the anchor, though
Back from the depths I was myself about
To touch my hands to sailors, reaching out,
And was devoured. A huge and savage beast
Swallowed me; sailors raised the half, released
Down to the navel, dead weight, nothing more,
The rest the shark bit off. So on this shore
I stay, my friend, and won't go home, for whom
They put the gruesome remnants in this tomb.

X

If my tombstone lies so low over me,
And is so small, oh passerby, to see,
    Still praise you should confer
    On Philainís, dear sir,
  For she her minstrel locust, who
  Before walked on the thorns, loved two
    Whole years, and now bereft
    Of my song clatter, left
My body not, but buried me, and made
This marker for the many songs I played.

XI

Happily down the road to Hades go,
  Not rough, curved, or uneven, but
Quite straight, sloped everywhere from high to low,
  And traveled even with eyes shut.

XII

"Like vine to pole, I'm propped up by my cane;
Death calls me down to Hades. Do not feign
  Deafness, my friend!
  Will you extend
Your happiness, if three years or if four
You warm yourself beneath the sun still more?"
  And saying so,
  No braggart, though
Quite old in years, he thrust his life away,
And with the greater number went to stay.

XIII

  Walk softly by the tomb, lest you
Would wake the surly wasp who, resting, dozes;

The anger of Hippónax, who
Snarled even at his parents, here reposes,
   In stillness gone to sleep just now.
Be careful, therefore, fit precaution take,
   For his impassioned words know how
Even in Hades to bring pain and heartache.

XIV

From Leonídas, homeless and hard-pressed,
And with a poor-provisioned flour chest,
Accept these offerings, Lathría. Take
Some precious olive oil, rich barley cake,
This green fig culled from the branch, five grapes that are
Of a well-wined bunch, from the bottom of a jar
An offering of drink. If, just as you
Have rescued me from sickness, so now too
My hateful poverty you could relieve,
A sacrifice of goat you will receive.

XV

A needy mother gives a cheap sketch to
Lord Bacchus, of her Míkythos. May you,
Oh Bacchus, lift him. If cheap be the gift,
Such are the offerings of straitened thrift.

XVI

Deft Théris, dexterous of hand, presented
Athena with his measuring rod, undented,
   An ax and plane with frame well fit,
   An augur with rotating bit,
And his curve-handled saw with straightened blade,
When he retired and ceased to ply his trade.

XVII

A well-curved hook, a line made of horsehair,
His long poles, and this weel contrived to snare
And shut free-swimmers in, discovery
Of men who cast nets, roaming round the sea;
Some fish-receiving baskets made of wicker;
Poseidon's spear—a trident, sharp fish-sticker;
And, taken from his boats, a twin oar-blade;
By custom to the patron of his trade
The fisherman Dióphantos imparted,
Remains of work that long ago he'd started.

XVIII

These gifts a man, called Dorieús the Smelly,
To Gluttony and Swilling dedicated:
Large kettles from Larissa with round belly,
And clay pots; a flesh hook, well-bent, brass-plated;
Soup-stirring ladle, grating knife for cheese,
And wide-mouth drinking cup. But now that you've
Received bad things from a bad giver, please
Don't ever temperance or self-restraint approve.

XIX

Not mine, these spoils. Who hung on cornice stones
Of Ares' shrine such thankless thanks? The cones
Of helms are whole, the shields are bloodless, bright;
The spear shafts are unbroken and too light.
With shame my whole face blushes, and the sweat
Pours from my brow, drips on my breast. Come let
The courtyard with such things, the colonnade,
The banquet hall and bedroom be arrayed,
But in horse-driving Ares' shrine reside
The bloody spoils! With those I'm satisfied.

XX

Cold water from two rocks cascading out,
   Wood statues—rustic offering
   To nymphs, and boulders of the spring,
Farewell! Your votive figures placed about,

Oh maidens, in the water moistened through,
   Farewell! I give as gift this cup,
   Which I, Aristoklés, drew up
When I dipped down to quench my thirst, to you.

XXI

With pillager of pasture, men, and cattle,
A beast who from dog barking did not flee,
Euálkes tending sheep one night did battle,
And slew and hung it on this stone-pine tree.

XXII

A solitary lion in full flight
From driving hail and snow one winter night,
Escaping from a frozen mountain peak,
Already pained in every limb and weak,
Came to the fold of goatherds, lovers of
Steep ridges. They sat down, and called above
To Zeus their savior, caring not the least
About the goats but for themselves. The beast
Then all night waited for the tempest's ending,
And not a single man or goat offending,
Departed. So to Zeus the mountain folk
This painting of their feat put on this oak.

XXIII

Oh you from town who walk this track
To fields, or from the fields come back,
This one is Hercules, and me,
I'm Hermes here, just as you see,
Two watchmen of the boundary line,
Our ears to men glad to incline;
But when you leave wild pears nearby,
He gobbles up the whole supply,
The same with grapes, it doesn't matter,
Ripe or not, heaped on the platter,
He takes everything that's there.
I hate it when we have to share,
It's just no fun. When someone brings
To both of us some offerings,
Let him not give in common; say
"To Hercules this I convey,"
But "This to Hermes I extend,"
And our contention he would end.

XXIV

  See how the old man has just tripped
     Himself from drinking, see
     Anacreon, how he
  Drags on his robe, whose hem has slipped

Down to his feet; and keeping even so
One slipper, though the other he's let go,

  He strikes his lyre and sings to all
     Of Báthyllos, or of
     Fair Megisteús his love.
  Watch, Bacchus, that he does not fall!

XXV

Hunt well beneath two hills, chaser of hare!
And if pursuing birds with lime and snare
    You come, from tall
    Embankment call
To me, Pan, forest watchman, and I too
With dogs and fowler rods will hunt with you.

XXVI

A bearded, full-grown spouse of a she-goat
Once in a vineyard gobbled down his throat
All of a vine's soft shoots, but a great sound
Called out to him "You bastard!" from the ground,
"Cut with your jaws my tendrils that bear fruit,
Yet steadfast in the earth again my root
Will make sweet nectar, plenty to suffice
To pour on you, goat, at your sacrifice!"

XXVII

Don't waste away by dragging out the year
    Wandering all about,
Off, my friend, to another land from here.
    Don't wear yourself out,

But let a wooden hut however plain,
    A small fire burning low
Give roof and warmth, if even from poor grain
    You'd have spare cake, with dough

Hand-kneaded in a hollow stone, and could
    With thyme but make your spread,
With pennyroyal or sharp salt, which would
    Be sweet when mixed with bread.

XXVIII

Flee from my cabin, dark-abiding mice!
The chest of Leonídas won't suffice
To nourish you; the old man can be fed
From his own means by salt and some coarse bread,
Contented like his fathers with this keep.
So why, then, do you excavate so deep
Within this nook, oh mouse who licks and laps?
You won't be tasting after-dinner scraps!
Speed to some other houses, where you'll dine
On fuller rations—there's not much in mine.

XXIX

   For sailing it's the hour,
   The meadows are in flower,
The chattering swallow now comes near,
The pleasant zephyr, too, is here,

   And silent is the sea,
   Once shaken violently
By waves and savage winds. May you
The anchors weigh and lines undo,

   Oh sailor, and let fly
   The full sail! These things, I,
Priapus, harbor god, command,
So you may trade in every land.

XXX

Here Deinoménes on this wall put me,
Priapus, so that, wakeful, I would be
A watchman of his garden. Look, thief, see
How far I stick out. You ask, "Is this true?
So far, just for these few greens?" For these few!

EXPLANATORY NOTES

I (GP 18, AP 7.656)

In this first of two epitaphs on abandoned graves that I have selected, the tomb of "wretched" Alkimenes is at pains to tell the passerby that it was once clearly visible, though now covered with weeds and bramble. The poem cleverly adopts the convention of the talking grave common in earlier Greek inscriptions, in which the tombstone addresses the passerby, telling him of the circumstances of the life and death of the deceased. Needless to say, this poem cannot have been an actual inscription, a circumstance that gives the epigram a subtle irony typical of much of Leonidas's work. The effective repetition of the name Alkimenes at the beginning and end of the poem poignantly reinforces the identification of the grave mound, which is otherwise almost unrecognizable. The reading of the last line is disputed. Some scholars take it to say that the bushes on which Alkimenes once waged war have now invaded his tomb in revenge, an imaginative reconstruction having nothing to do with the spirit of the poem. Much like the other characters in Leonidas's poetry, Alkimenes is a peasant, not a proud warrior; his grave is a "little tomb," not a grand monument. I have adopted what seems to me the more likely reading of Geffcken.

II (GP 73, AP 7.478)

The grave in this poem is near a highway and has been disturbed by passing traffic. The deceased again is presumably poor, probably living in the countryside and without relatives to care for his tomb. In contrast to the first poem, the name of the deceased is not given in this epigram. The absence of a name is rare in Hellenistic poetry about the dead, which often included even patronymics to give the impression of actual inscriptions (see VIII and IX). The omission here increases the impression of hopeless neglect.

III (GP 14, AP 7.665)

Hesiod, writing in *Works and Days* four hundred years before Leonidas, says that we should praise a small ship but put our goods in a big one. This poem says that even the largest ship is no match for a squall. Advice not to take to sea is a common theme in Greek literature, and after the first two lines we expect death by drowning. What we do not anticipate is that the body will have been washed onto the shore and given a proper burial, so important to the Greeks (and still to us now). This slight variation upon a common theme may have seemed unanticipated and witty to many of Leonidas's readers, though the humor is perhaps more difficult for us now to appreciate.

IV (GP 20, AP 7.295)

The next two poems I have included are about humble working people adept at their trade, who lived decently and died at great old age. The fisherman of this poem could swim better than a gull and is said *not* to have died from a storm at sea, a reversal of the common theme of drowned sailors (as in the preceding poem). Arcturus is one of the brightest stars in the sky in the constellation Boötes, the Plowman. Its conspicuous rising in autumn marked the end of the safest season for sailing in the Mediterranean. Instead of shipwreck, the fisherman died of old age, *automatos,* "with no clear cause," and "out like a lamp." He lived and died in his little hut apparently without family and was buried by his fellow fishermen. The Greek word *thiasos* used by Leonidas can mean simply a group of associates but can also have the more formal meaning of a private organization such as a guild. The circumstances of the burial are an indication both of the fisherman's poverty and of the generosity of the honest poor.

V (GP 72, AP 7.726)

This is one of Leonidas's most admired poems. Spinning and weaving were the constant occupation of women in ancient Greece, even in rich households. Penelope, wife of Ulysses, famously wove a shroud for her father-in-law Laertes during the day, and then every night undid what she had woven to postpone choosing a suitor. The weaver of this poem was from a much lower class, rising early and weaving far into the night to keep poverty away, singing until dawn around "the long course of Athena." Athena was the goddess of spinning and weaving, and her "long course" was the loom. The adjective "beautiful" in the last line could be taken to refer to the cloth being woven, but I have again followed Geffcken and taken it to modify the woman herself, who two lines earlier is also described as "lovely." It may seem surprising that Leonidas would have spoken of an elderly woman in this way, but it is not so much her physical appearance as her grace and contentment that evoke his praise. For the river Acheron, see note to Anyte I.

VI (GP 68, AP 7.455)

This poem is not an epitaph—no family would have placed a drinking cup on top of the grave of a bibulous woman—but is instead an early example of an invective epigram written to criticize or make fun, not of an actual person but rather of a type of person. It is satire with an ethical message, like the *spoudaiogelion* of the Cynics. The woman drunkard was a stock character of comedy and appears with some regularity in Greek (and Latin) literature. The name Maronis is clearly fictitious and may be related to the Maron of the *Odyssey*, a priest of Apollo who provided the wine used to lull to sleep the Cyclops Polyphemus. Epigrams like this, though rare among the poems of Meleager's *Garland*, became increasingly common in later centuries and constitute the great majority of the epigrams of Lucillius (see chapter 10).

VII *(GP 67, AP 7.452)*

Now instead of drunkenness it is temperance that provides the joke. Let's drink and be merry, since Euboulos for all his moderation and sobriety still went to Hades, as all of us must. Hades here is used (as often) for the realm of the underworld rather than its ruler. In Greek the name Euboulos means "prudent," and the poet may have used it to represent a type of person (as in VI) rather than for anyone in particular. But it is possible that the Euboulos of the poem is the third-century BCE author of *The Sale of Diogenes,* a book containing stories about the life of the famous Cynic philosopher Diogenes and advice from a Cynic perspective on the raising of children. Regardless of how we are meant to identify Euboulos, the epigram contains implied but unmistakable criticism of the extreme asceticism of Diogenes and his followers.

VIII *(GP 66, AP 7.504)*

The next two poems are humorous anecdotes, with perhaps some basis in fact. This poem about a fisherman—"whom none could surpass"— again emphasizes his skillfulness. Wrasses are one of the largest families of marine fishes, many of which are brightly colored and prized as aquarium specimens. The "fateful threads of doom" are the threads of the three Fates or Moirai, who spin the thread of life for each person and cut it off at death. Parmis "filled up" his threads, meaning he used them up and came to the end of his life. As in IV, the fisherman is buried by a friend rather than by members of his family. With "the fisher Fischer" I have tried to reproduce the poem's *Gripon ho gripeus,* the latter a variant of the former and both meaning "fisherman."

IX (GP 65, AP 7.506)

This, like epigram I, is a first-person narration with a first name and patronymic as in many actual inscriptions. But the story it tells is so bizarre that it can only be book poetry. The name of the sailor also suggests its purely literary nature: Tharsys means "bold" or "courageous," in this case overly so. It would have taken a big shark to take half of a man in a single bite, but the loss of entire limbs was common then as now. The Ionian Sea is that part of the Mediterranean lying between western Greece and southern Italy and Sicily. I have translated the Greek word *pristis* as "shark," since this is the only marine animal that would have undertaken such an attack; the exact meaning of this word is disputed, however, and it is sometimes taken to mean "sawfish" (from the Greek *prion,* meaning "saw").

X (GP 21, AP 7.198)

This poem purports to be an epitaph for the tiny tombstone of a locust, who was a pet of the girl Philainis. The poem was clearly patterned after Anyte IX. Adult locusts generally live only a few months during the summer season, though some can live as long as a year. The life span of an adult grasshopper or cricket is usually even shorter. Thus the *akris* of Philainis is unlikely to have lived in captivity for "two whole years," nor indeed is a young girl likely to have paid attention to an insect for so long. These details add to the exaggerated tone of the poem, which (unlike Anyte's poem) is humorous rather than touching or sympathetic.

XI (GP 79)

A restating of a maxim of Bion, an itinerant Cynic philosopher and preacher and a contemporary of Leonidas: "The road to Hades is easy; at least we leave for it with eyes closed."

XII (GP 78, AP 7.731)

Another poem about death heavily influenced by Cynic philosophy. Bion taught that a body worn out by old age should be abandoned like a decrepit house—essentially, the advice of the poem, given by one old man to another. For the Greeks "the greater number" were the dead, whose sum was imagined to be larger than that of the people then alive.

XIII (GP 58, AP 7.408)

This epitaph is clearly epideictic and one of a large number of fictitious Hellenistic epitaphs of Greek poets (see also XXIV and Theocritus V and XII). Hipponax was a sixth-century iambic poet from the Ionian (now Turkish) city of Ephesus, who wrote invective and parody. He is known for his poetry of violent personal abuse, particularly of the two sculptors Boupalos and Athenis, who are said to have made caricatures of the poet's ugly appearance. One fragment of Hipponax says "hold my cloak and I'll knock out the eye of Boupalos"; in another, Boupalos is accused of sleeping with his mother.

XIV (GP 36, AP 6.300)

Just as Leonidas used epitaphs to write generally about death in all its forms rather than to produce actual inscriptions, so he exploited the dedication epigram for many different purposes. Like Anyte, he often wrote about people of humble means. In this the first of the dedication epigrams I have selected, Leonidas himself offers a few simple but treasured items of food and drink to Lathria—apparently Aphrodite, a goddess otherwise little in evidence in his poetry. Like the weaver of epigram V, the poet is afraid to be poor, and this apprehension distinguishes him from a true Cynic (see introduction to this chapter).

XV *(GP 39, AP 6.355)*

The mother in this epigram is destitute but nevertheless dedicates a portrait to Bacchus of her son Mikythos, with a plea that the god help him. The name, like the Mikkos of Callimachus III and Theocritus III (see chapters 6 and 7), means "little one" and may be a baby name or nickname.

XVI *(GP 7, AP 6.204)*

In the next two epigrams I have included, workmen upon retirement dedicate the tools of their livelihood. Leonidas used the form of a dedication epigram to express his admiration of the skill and competence of a common laborer, much as in epitaphs IV and V. The carpenter is *daidalocheir,* clever with his hands, or "deft" and "dexterous." Though clearly from the lower classes, the man evidently took pride in the implements of his craft.

XVII *(GP 52, AP 6.4)*

A fisherman dedicates his tools "to the patron of his trade"—presumably a deity, though the identity of the god is unclear. A "weel" is a kind of trap made from wicker and used in swiftly moving currents; fish were swept in and couldn't swim back out. Tridents appear to have been used primarily in fishing at night.

XVIII *(GP 56, AP 6.305)*

A gourmand dedicates cooking utensils to the gods Gluttony and Swilling in the hope of keeping temperance at bay. This poem displays the same love of lists as do XVI and XVII, but the poet makes no attempt to engage our interest or sympathy. Rather, like VI, the poem is humorous invective influenced by the Cynics, who made temperance a byword. The Dorieus of the poem may have been an actual person, a poet said to have written a poem about the voraciousness of the athlete Milon (on whom see Lucillius VIII and note). That Leonidas would have written a poem about the gluttony of someone who himself wrote a poem about a glutton is perfectly consistent with everything we know about the practice of poets in the third century BCE.

XIX (GP 25, AP 9.322)

The war god Ares complains of the unused condition of the implements of battle hung in his shrine. Some scholars, seeking an historical explanation for this poem, view it as pointed criticism by Leonidas of the cowardice of his countrymen. There is, however, no evidence of fainthearted-ness among either the citizens of Tarentum or the soldiers of the Greek general Pyrrhus whose army defended Tarentum. Pyrrhus's soldiers were so famous for dying in large numbers at the hands of the Romans in the battle of Asculum in 279 BCE that from them comes our phrase "Pyrrhic victory." It is probably more fruitful to see this epigram as an exercise in genre, as an "antidedication." Instead of the dedicator speaking and listing the gifts he is giving to the god, it is the god himself who speaks. And instead of the customary prayer at the end asking the god or goddess to accept the gifts and to give meet recompense, the god complains of the unsuitability of the gifts and in effect rejects them. This was an influential poem, later imitated by Meleager as well as by Antipater of Sidon and Leonidas of Alexandria.

XX (GP 5, AP 9.326)

In this first of three poems on rural subjects that I have selected from the many Leonidas wrote, a traveler named Aristokles dedicates his drinking cup to the nymphs of a country spring. Near enough to the stream to be splashed by the waters are rustic wooden statues and votive figures, probably of wax or terra-cotta, dedicated to the nymphs by shepherds or previous visitors. This poem was modeled on epigram XI of Anyte, also a dedication in part to nymphs at a rustic spring.

XXI *(GP 48, AP 6.262)*

A shepherd named Eualkes hangs up on a tree the corpse or skin of a marauding animal. The poem celebrates the valor of the shepherd, who even in the dark of night slew a wolf or bear or lion fierce enough to be unfazed by the barking of dogs. Since the hanging up of an offering is a normal way of honoring a god, the poem has the form of a dedication. The beast is not identified, and for a real inscription, with the animal in full view, such identification would not have been necessary. It is a bit odd, however, that no god is mentioned; this omission leaves us free to wonder if the poem was written to accompany a painting with a rural setting or was purely epideictic, a narrative on a pastoral theme.

XXII *(GP 53, AP 6.221)*

Goatherds, unexpectedly spared from injury by a lion, dedicate to Zeus a painting of their ordeal. This is a remarkably vivid poem, which tells a story sufficiently plausible to be based on an actual occurrence. Although considerably less valorous than the Eualkes of the preceding poem, the goatherds nevertheless evoke our sympathy and our relief at their miraculous delivery.

XXIII *(GP 27, AP 9.316)*

An epideictic poem about a double herm or boundary marker. The Greeks often used a bust or small statue of Hermes or another god or hero to mark a boundary—especially between cities and territories, but also sometimes between private holdings. The statue of the poem is presumably a double herm of two gods back to back, placed near a well-used path or road. The offerings to the statue are simple fare from rustic peasants, and it is amusing to think of the two herms arguing with one another like children about which one got the larger portion. Hercules had a reputation in antiquity as a glutton, also exploited by Callimachus in his *Hymn to Artemis*. The reading of the epigram is disputed, with many scholars postulating a gap in the text after line 5 (line 6 of my translation). The flow of the poem does seem a little disrupted at this point, but I have adopted the suggestion of Wilamowitz (*Hellenistische Dichtung* 2:110) and taken the poem to be complete with his emendation.

XXIV (GP 90, APl 307)

A portrait of the sixth-century Greek lyric poet Anacreon, written either to accompany a statue of the poet or, more likely, as an ecphrasis or description of a statue such as the one known to have been erected at Teos (see Theocritus XII) or on the Acropolis in Athens. Many fragments and a few possibly complete poems have survived by Anacreon, whose most common themes were wine, love of boys, and song (see chapter 1). Bacchus, as the god of wine and with some responsibility for Anacreon's plight, is asked in the last line to help keep him upright. The epigram displays evident sympathy of one poet for another, even though the two appear to have had very different interests and temperaments. Bathyllos and Megisteus are lovers praised by Anacreon in his poetry.

XXV (GP 29, AP 9.337)

Another epigram of the countryside, similar in spirit and rustic setting to Anyte XI but emphasizing the role of Pan as a protector of forest huntsmen rather than as a god of shepherds. The poem was well-known in antiquity and translated nearly word for word into Latin by Propertius (3.13.43–46). The birdlime mentioned in line 2 is a mixture of substances such as mistletoe berries and holly bark, boiled down to form a sticky amalgam. This was then spread on the "fowler rods" to entrap the birds.

XXVI (GP 32, AP 9.99)

A poem again well-known in antiquity, whose last line has survived in a house on the Via Stabiana at Pompeii, where it appears as a part of an inscription on a fresco showing a goat eating vine leaves. The tale of the goat and the vine is from Aesop. Leonidas may have been the first of the third-century poets to write epigrams on fables. In the same way that many of his poems describe the life of humble workmen instead of heroes or kings, his poems can encompass the lower genre of folktales without referring to any of the better known Greek myths.

XXVII (GP 33, AP 7.736)

This and the following poem are clear examples of epideictic poems on moral themes; apparently the first epigrams of their kind, they are related to the famous poem of Martial on the simple life (10.47), written almost four centuries later. That Leonidas lived the life of an exile is also indicated in an epitaph for him, which begins

> Far from my home of Italy I lie;
> This is to me more bitter than to die.

The poet's homily of self-sufficiency and the simple life reflects a Cynic influence, though the exhortation to stay in one place doesn't. The most famous Cynic philosophers such as Diogenes, Crates, and Bion all traveled extensively from city to city to lecture throughout the Greek world. When Diogenes was asked of what *polis* or city he was the *polites* or citizen, he replied that he was a citizen of the world, *kosmopolites*—from which we get our word "cosmopolitan." Leonidas might have given the same response but with sadness rather than with pride. Pennyroyal is an herb related to mint; as well as for seasoning, the ancients used it for medicinal purposes and even as a flea repellent.

XXVIII (GP 37, AP 6.302)

The poet tells mice to leave his cottage since they will find nothing to eat in his poor abode. The word *autarkes* or "self-sufficient," which Leonidas uses to describe himself in the poem and which I have translated as "from his own means," was another Cynic byword, whose importance Diogenes is said to have learned by observing the behavior of a mouse. Leonidas goes on to say, however, that he is "contented like his fathers with this keep," suggesting to the Italian scholar Gigante that the ideal of a frugal and temperate life expressed in this and other poems might have been influenced less by the Cynics than by the poet's presumably Spartan upbringing—Tarentum was founded by settlers from ancient Sparta. The theme of this poem is inverted with humorous effect in Lucillius XXVII.

XXIX and XXX (GP 85, AP 10.1 and GP 83, APl 236)

These are two of the earliest epigrams on Priapus, a minor god in the Greek pantheon who first appeared in Greek literature in the fourth century BCE. Priapus is the god of fertility and the guardian of harbors and gardens, always depicted with a pronounced and erect phallus. Poem XXIX was much imitated, cited by Cicero and probably also known to Catullus, whose poem 46 on the coming of spring begins in a similar way. Poem XXX and other later epigrams that resemble it had a direct influence on the Priapean poems of Martial, as well as on the unknown poet or poets of the *Corpus Priapeorum,* a collection of about eighty short poems in Latin on Priapus probably written during the middle or end of the first century CE. Many of the poems of the *Corpus* are strikingly similar in theme and mood to Leonidas's poem, with Priapus himself speaking and often referring to his function as a custodian of the garden. There is also often explicit reference in Latin Priapean poetry to the phallus of the god and a threat of reprisal directed at anyone who invades the garden precincts. The ending of Leonidas's poem has what is usually called "point"; that is, the argument of the poem is brought to its conclusion in the last line or even the last word, often with a sudden and witty turn of phrase, much like a bon mot. Most of his other epigrams do not do this; and point, though present in some third-century Greek epigrams, is by no means as common as it would later become in Lucillius (see chapter 10) and then in Martial.

CHAPTER FOUR

Asclepiades

Asclepiades is one of the most interesting and appealing figures of the third century. Among the first of the Hellenistic poets to write love epigrams, he helped turn a genre consisting mostly of epitaphs and dedications into a personal form of expression with many of the hallmarks of lyric poetry. The invention of the love epigram had an enormous effect on the development of Greek verse in the Hellenistic era, and much later on the Latin love poetry of Catullus and the elegists Propertius, Tibullus, and Ovid. Although Asclepiades wrote traditional dedication epigrams and epitaphs, it was his love epigrams that had the greatest influence; many of the other Greek poets of the third century imitated the themes and even the wording of his poetry.

Asclepiades was probably a contemporary of Anyte, older than Calli-machus, and spoken of as if already an established figure by Theocritus. Theocritus tells us that Asclepiades came from the island of Samos in Ionia, off the western coast of what is now Turkey. It is likely that Asclepiades was personally acquainted with many of the other third-century poets, and since both Posidippus and Callimachus lived for much of their lives in Alexandria and frequented the royal court, Asclepiades too probably spent at least a part of his life in the Egyptian capital. One of his epigrams was apparently written in praise of a mistress of Ptolemy Philadelphus (see XVII and note), and it is unlikely that Asclepiades would have written a poem like this unless he had known Ptolemy rather well.

Asclepiades lived at least into his fifties, since he received honorary citizenship in Delphi in 275 BCE. He seems therefore to have had a long and illustrious career, and his extant poems doubtless represent only a fraction of his total output. He was called by one ancient scholar an *epi-grammatographos,* or "writer of epigrams," and from him—unlike Theocritus or Callimachus—we have no undisputed examples of any other kind of poem. It is nevertheless possible that Asclepiades did at times write in a different style, since a metrical form not used in his epigrams (the Asclepiad) was apparently named after him; it would have been odd if he himself had not used this meter, but we have no idea what he might have written in it.

Of the epigrams of Asclepiades that have survived, the great majority are about love. Asclepiades presents us with a catalogue of lovers in all of their variety, mostly heterosexual but a few involving male couples and even one rather disapproving epigram about love between women. These poems present lovers at the very beginning of their attraction, well into their affair, and at its end. Lovers are occasionally happy but are more often disappointed; in several poems they are refused entry standing on the threshold of the house of the beloved. We encounter virgins hesitant before their first sexual experience and seasoned professionals. Many of the women in his poems are probably meant to be prostitutes or courtesans, but in other epigrams they seem to be just ordinary women, pursuing and pursued.

The variety of love in all of its forms is mirrored by a variety of mood. Some poems are flippant and fun, but others are serious and purport to express deep personal feeling (for example XIII and XV). The language of the poems is usually simple, almost conversational, unlike the often convoluted expression in Leonidas and many later poets of Greek epigrams. But this simplicity can be deceptive: these are beautifully constructed poems in which not a single word is wasted. Asclepiades was a master at setting the scene of the poem with just a few opening words. We find ourselves with Hermione in her bedroom as she is undressing, or outside Pythias's door, or in a tavern with the poet and a drinking companion. The endings are also carefully crafted, occasionally with some surprising feature reserved for the last line or even the last word. It was perhaps the intrinsic brevity of epigrams that encouraged Asclepiades to write his love poems in this compressed style, but he gave a much greater attention to the beginnings and endings of his poems than did Anyte or Leonidas.

Another characteristic of the poems of Asclepiades is their freedom of expression and flexible syntax. Many of the epigrams of the third-century Greeks are organized rhetorically, relying on parallel structure, conditional sentences, and antithesis, often reinforced by verbal repetition. These features may come from short elegy, particularly from poetry attributed to Theognis (see chapter 1). The love poetry of Asclepiades, on the other hand, is often in quite a different style, containing many short sentences or longer sentences broken up into shorter units. Imperatives and questions are much more common and are often placed in the middle of a verse. Parallel structure and antithesis are certainly present (see, for example, the ending of epigram XV), but far more often Asclepiades strings together several short statements (for example, in XVI), giving his poems an attractive informality. We shall find many of these same features in the epigrams of the other Greek love poets, and they show up several centuries later in the poetry of Latin poets like Catullus.

So far as we can tell, no one before Asclepiades wrote love poetry in this way. The famous poem of Sappho "He seems to me as fortunate as the gods," one of the masterpieces of Greek lyric, is more discursive and has much longer syntactical units. It is consequently more formal, and more serious and moving. Asclepiades, in contrast, uses brevity and a conversational ease of expression to produce poems that are iridescent, with a surprising diversity of emotion and language—often amusing, sometimes poignant, but never banal or boring. He is by universal ac-knowledgment a master of the love epigram and one of the most impor-tant poets of the Hellenistic era.

I

Eight cubits keep away, inclement sea.
Swell and cry out, you'll get no good from me
By pulling down my tomb with your great wave:
You'll find but bones and ashes in my grave.

II

Oh you, my empty barrow who pass by,
When next in Chios, tell my father I
Was wracked by storm, of ship and goods bereft,
And only Eúhippos, my name, is left.

III ·

Once Kónnaros wrote such a pretty hand,
He vanquished all the other schoolboys, and
    Got eighty knucklebones as prize.
Then me, gift to the Muses, he hung here,
A comic mask of old man Chares, near
    The other children's claps and cries.

IV

To you, Love, Lysidíkë dedicates
Her golden riding spur, with which she breaks
In many a supine horse, so lightly led
That never does her pretty thigh turn red.
Since spurless she still makes the finish line,
She hangs her golden gear up in your shrine.

V

Sweet is cold drink to thirst in summer, sweet
Are stars of spring to sailors, but one sheet
That covers lovers lying side by side
Is sweeter still, and Love is glorified.

VI

    I tire of living, not yet twenty-two.
           Oh Cupids, why
This plague? Why do you burn me? If I die,
         What will you do?
    It's clear, Cupids, you'll stay the same,
Heedlessly playing your knucklebones game.

VII

This residue of soul, whatever it be,
Let it at least have some tranquillity,
Or do not, Cupids, strike with arrows still,
But, by the gods, with thunderbolts, until
I am but ash and cinder. Strike your blow,
Yes, Cupids, yes! I'm shriveled up with woe,
And if there's anything at all from you
That I can have, it's this I'd have you do.

VIII

Dórkion wants to set young men on fire,
Knows how to shoot off quick darts of desire
   Just like a tender boy,
   Lewd love they all enjoy,
So in felt hat, lust flashing from her eyes,
She lets her cloak reveal her naked thighs.

IX

Bittó and Nánnion are two
Samian women, women who
Wish not to visit Love's domains
By rules the goddess preordains,
Deserting her prescribed delight
For other joys that are not right.
Hate, Aphrodite, those who've fled
From your dominion's marriage bed!

X

You save yourself, but why? For when you go
To Hades, girl, you won't find love below.
The living have love's pleasures; when we die,
As bones and ashes, maiden, we shall lie.

XI

   I call to witness only you:
   See, Night, what Pythiás can do,
How she mistreats and tricks her paramour.
   Invited, not uncalled I came;
   May she, enduring just the same,
Complain to you later, standing at my door.

XII

Bring lightning, thunder, hail and snow,
Bring darkness, all the black clouds throw
Down to the earth, and if I die
Then, Zeus, you'll stop me. But if I
Can live, beset by worse than these,
Then I shall revel as I please.
A god more powerful than you
Compels me, Zeus, the same god who
Got you to be a golden shower,
Once slipping through a brazen tower.

XIII

Hang here, my garlands, by the double door,
Don't let your shaken leaves fall to the floor,
Those leaves I moistened with a lover's tears;
But when the door swings out and he appears,
Then sprinkle on his head my weeping rain,
That his blond hair may drink my drops of pain.

XIV

Wine is the test of love. What he denied,
The many toasts we made have verified,
As weeping, nodding low, he hid his face,
And his garland, tightly bound, slipped out of place.

XV

Once Archeádes was beset with yearning,
    But now, poor me, won't look my way,
    Not even just to tease or play.
Not always sweet is honeyed Love, but turning
    Tormentful, can for lovers be
    Often a sweeter deity.

XVI

By holy Demeter, the famed Nikó
Swore she would come just after dark, and so
She's not here, it's the middle of the night.
Was this on purpose? Boys, put out the light!

XVII

Didýme's bloom has put me in her power;
    I melt with desire,
    Like wax by the fire,
When I behold, alas, her youthful flower.

If she is black, who cares? So too is coal,
    But put in the flame
    It glows red, the same
As roses when their petals first unroll.

XVIII

With winsome Hermióne once I played,
Whose many-colored panties were arrayed
With golden letters, "Always love me, do,
But don't fret if another holds me too."

XIX

If you had wings, and in your hand
    Some arrows and a bow,
Not Cupid as the son of Venus,
    Boy, but you we'd know.

XX

Drink up, Asclepiádes, why these tears?
What's wrong? You aren't the only one who fears
That hard Love's made him captive, or can claim
Alone that bitter Cupid's taken aim
With bow and arrows. Why then do you make
Yourself but living ashes? Let us take
Our Bacchus straight, a finger-length of day
Is all that lingers. Or should we delay
And wait once more to see the daylight's end,
The bedtime lamp? Let's drink, my forlorn friend,
For not much time is left to interpose,
Before our day with one long night will close.

EXPLANATORY NOTES

I (GP 30, AP 7.284)

Eight cubits is a little less than 4 meters. The poem tells the sea it can
bluster all it wants but to keep its distance, since there is nothing in the
grave worth taking. The antipathy shown by the deceased for the sea
suggests that the grave is meant to be that of a drowned sailor whose
body was recovered and buried on land. No sailor having found a rest-
ing place on the shore would want his bones pulled back into the deep.

II (GP 31, AP 7.500)

This is an epitaph for a cenotaph, or empty grave. Because a proper
burial had such significance, an epitaph for an empty grave mourns not
only the death of the person whose name is given but also the absence
of proper burial rites. The dead man is Euhippos from the island of
Chios off the western coast of Turkey, a merchant lost at sea with his

ship and merchandise. We are left to wonder who set up this tomb or would even have known of Euhippos's death, if the ship with all of its cargo was lost.

III (GP 27, AP 6.308)

One of the few dedication epigrams among the surviving poems of Asclepiades. We are meant to imagine a schoolboy winning a prize for writing or penmanship. Knucklebones, originally from sheep, were used like dice or jacks in a variety of children's games. A game for which we have a written description used only four or five, so eighty would seem a rather large number. That knucklebones are the prize suggests that the children were young. "Old man Chares" was presumably a character in a play, perhaps an irascible old man, though this name does not occur in any surviving Greek comedy. Some scholars have proposed that the dedication is of a clay figure rather than a mask—the Greek is not entirely clear on the nature of the object. A mask seems more likely, however, since in an epigram Callimachus wrote in imitation (XVI)— also of a dedication to the Muses by a schoolboy, also of an object placed in a classroom amid the din of the students—the object dedicated is clearly a mask, though predictably Callimachus makes it tragic instead of comic.

IV (GP 6, AP 5.203)

Asclepiades may have been the first (but was certainly not the last) to write an erotic epigram in the form of a mock dedication. Lysidike, a courtesan, is clearly successful if she is rich enough to own and even dedicate a large piece of gold jewelry like a spur. Of the woman's *modus amandi,* Horace in *Satires* 2 (7.49–50) speaks of a wanton prostitute who sets a supine horse in motion with her buttocks, though there is no mention of a spur. Perhaps, like Lysidike, she had dedicated it when she no longer needed it. Some scholars think that *akentetos* at the end of the poem means not "spurless" but "unspurred" or "ungoaded"; Pindar uses the word in this way. That would, however, require the man and woman to change places, an awkward reversal of motif for which there is no other indication in the poem. I have adopted the reading of Alan Cameron (in *Callimachus and His Critics*) and Kathryn Gutzwiller (in *Poetic Garlands*), which seems to me a more natural interpretation.

V (GP 1, AP 5.169)

One of only a few poems by Asclepiades about lovers who are happy. The lovers are collectively given in the male gender in Greek, which could mean either that both are male or that one is male and one female. The poem begins with a list called a priamel, consisting of what the poet isn't going to say or doesn't favor and serving as a foil for his own choice or preference (see also Callimachus XXI and Philodemos XVII). The comparison of drink to the thirsty and clear skies to sailors may have been borrowed from Aeschylus (*Agamemnon* 899–901). Spring stars are sweet to sailors, because sailors avoided the Mediterranean during the winter and could begin sailing only when spring had come (see Leonidas IV and XXIX). The reference to cool drink in summer reminds us of Anyte XIV and XV, in which the traveler also in summer is urged to satisfy his thirst at a country spring. If, as Gutzwiller has suggested, Anyte's poems served as a programmatic introduction to her book of poetry, Asclepiades' poem may be performing a similar function. He may be saying that though the poetry of Anyte is sweet, his love poetry is even sweeter.

VI (GP 15, AP 12.46)

The sentiment of this epigram, dramatically different from that of the preceding poem, is much more typical of Asclepiades' verse. Love is a game of chance played by whimsical gods and has no winners. For knucklebones, see the note to Asclepiades III. This poem may have been influenced by Anacreon (fr. 398), "Knucklebones are the mad passion and battle din of Eros [i.e., Cupid]." See also Meleager XI. The present poem displays stylistic features characteristic of Asclepiades' poetry, including vocatives and address by the poet to himself or someone else, and a conversational syntax, often accompanied by imperatives or (as here) short questions in the middle of the line. These elements give his poetry a liveliness suggestive of actual speech, which became characteristic of love epigram of the third-century poets.

VII (GP 17, AP 12.166)

The poem prays for some respite from love or, failing that, for death no matter how violent. We are perhaps meant to imagine the poet out on a revel or at the door of his beloved on a particularly stormy evening (see also XII). The language of the poem is intentionally melodramatic, almost humorously so. The "residue of soul" shows up later in an erotic epigram by Callimachus (XXII) as "half of my soul."

VIII (GP 20, AP 12.161)

An early example in Western literature of cross-dressing. Dorkion is a diminutive of the Greek word *dorkas,* meaning "deer" or "gazelle." She is often taken to be a prostitute with an unconventional approach to drumming up business, though it isn't terribly important for the poem whether she expected payment for her services. The *petasos* she wears is a broad-brimmed felt hat, so commonly worn by young men that it became almost a badge of their identity. Dorkion also wears a short military cloak called a *chlamys,* again often part of the uniform of Greek youths. The cloak was sufficiently short that it would have shown off her legs nicely as she strutted about.

IX (GP 7, AP 5.207)

Here we have two women from the island of Samos who prefer the company of other women to that of men. Women from Samos had a reputation for prostitution, and since Asclepiades also came from Samos, some scholars have speculated that he actually knew these women and that the poem reflects the slander of a disappointed lover. Taken as a whole, however, his collection of poems offers nearly a catalogue of women in different amatory situations. Such a review would have been incomplete without a female couple, and we are under no obligation to identify Bitto and Nannion with actual people.

X (GP 2, AP 5.85)

The Greek words used for "girl" and "maiden" indicate that the woman in this poem is a virgin. The view of death in the poem is typical of Greek epitaphs, which rarely speak of an afterlife in any way that is positive. Though Greek mystic religions imagined a congregation of the blessed something like a Christian paradise, such views were not widespread.

XI (GP 13, AP 5.164)

This poem is a *paraclausithyron*, to be recited at the door of the beloved. Though the lover has (or at least claims to have) an actual appointment, he is still left standing at the threshold. He prays to Night that the woman may later suffer the same fate (on this poem and its variation by Posidippus, see chapter 1).

XII (GP 11, AP 5.64)

Another *paraclausithyron,* this time addressed to Zeus, the god of light-
ning and thunder. The poet is again out on a *komos* (or revel) on a par-
ticularly nasty evening. The god who compels him is unnamed but
masculine and so must be Eros or Cupid rather than Aphrodite. The
myth alluded to at the end of the poem is that of Danae, who was locked
up in a bronze tower by her father, Acrisius, because an oracle had pre-
dicted that she would bear a son who would kill her father. Zeus turned
himself into a golden shower and penetrated the tower (and her), and she
later gave birth to the hero Perseus, slayer of Medusa and also of Acrisius,
just as the oracle had foretold.

XIII (GP 12, AP 5.145)

This final *paraclausithyron* for a boy or young man is one of the most
touching of Asclepiades' poems. The poet has apparently failed in his at
tempt to enter the house and hangs his garlands on the double door at the
threshold. There is a good description of this custom in *De Rerum Natura*
of Lucretius (4.1177–79): "But the lover shut out, weeping, often covers the
threshold with flowers and wreaths, anoints the proud doorposts with oil
of marjoram, presses his love-sick kisses upon the door" (trans. Rouse/
Smith, Loeb ed.). Similar garlands make their appearance in Ovid's
Metamorphoses (14.708–9), where Iphis hangs "garlands drenched with
the dew of tears" on the doorposts of his beloved Anaxarete.

XIV (GP 18, AP 12.135)

The scene of this epigram is a symposium, since the man is wearing a
garland. That wine reveals the truth of love (and of everything else) was
proverbial to the Greeks as well as to the Romans, who declared *in vino ver-
itas.* This poem was the model for Callimachus XXVIII (see chapter 1).

XV (GP 19, AP 12.153)

The Greek clearly indicates that the speaker in this poem is a woman and that Archeades is a man—this is difficult to indicate in English, since our adjectives do not reveal the gender of the nouns they modify. Thus we have a woman speaking about her male lover. Erotic epigrams written by a man from a woman's point of view are rare in Hellenistic poetry but perhaps not unexpected from Asclepiades, who includes such a broad range of amatory experience in his epigram collection. The logic of the poem seems faulty at first: if "honeyed love" is not always sweet, then we expect it "turning tormentful" to become *glykypikros* as Sappho put it, "bittersweet." That it can grow even sweeter takes us by surprise and gives poignancy to a commonplace.

XVI (GP 10, AP 5.150)

A woman breaks her promise. Swearing by Demeter seems to have been especially common among women. The "boys" are slave boys, who are asked to put out the light when the poet says he tires of waiting.

XVII (GP 5, AP 5.210)

The Didyme of this poem may be a Greek woman of dark complexion, but more likely she is a black woman, an Ethiopian or an Egyptian. Ptolemy Philadelphus (king of Egypt from 282 to 246 BCE) had an African mistress who was called Didyme, and Alan Cameron has suggested in "Two Mistresses of Ptolemy Philadelphus" that this poem is a poetic tribute to her. Other scholars have doubted that Asclepiades would have risked expressing sexual attraction to his ruler's girlfriend; but Asclepiades was probably over fifty when Ptolemy Philadelphus came to power, so when Asclepiades wrote this poem he may have been too old for anyone to take his claim of love to be anything other than a charming expression of admiration. Moreover, Asclepiades did write this poem, and since the woman is black and has the same name as Ptolemy's mistress, Asclepiades couldn't very well have said to his ruler "No, no, not *that* Didyme" and gotten away with it. It is equally possible, as Michael Haslam has pointed out to me, that the poem was not intended to be in the voice of the poet (see poem XV), but that Asclepiades may have written the epigram as if for Ptolemy himself to recite in praise of Didyme. The poem is practically the only evidence we have that Asclepiades was connected to the court in Alexandria and lived in Egypt for part of his life (see Cameron's article). The poet's clever description of the way the woman's glow of sexual excitement brightens into the red of a rosebud is certainly a compliment of the highest order. The reading "bloom" in line 1 is disputed by some scholars, who are inclined to substitute "eye"; that is, "Didyme's glance (or perhaps the beauty of her eyes) has put me in her power." But it is an important feature of the poem's construction that Didyme's bloom at the beginning of the poem turn into a rosebud at the end.

XVIII (GP 4, AP 5.158)

Hermione is usually assumed to be a prostitute warning her clientele not to be jealous, but she could equally well be an independent-minded (and sexually compliant) woman with more than one lover. The name Hermione appears at the beginning of book 4 of the *Odyssey,* where Helen and Menelaus are said to have a beautiful daughter of that name. I have translated the Greek word *zonion* as "panties," since the *zonion* was a women's lower undergarment whose loosening is often described in Greek literature as the last impediment to intercourse. I am taking some liberty in doing so, since Greek women did not, strictly speaking, wear panties, and the *zonion* was in fact a strip of cloth, often translated as "belt." This illustrates the translator's dilemma: a literal translation, though more faithful to the Greek, conveys nothing of the sexual innuendo the poet clearly intended.

XIX (GP 21, AP 12.75)

This poem could be amatory addressed to a handsome young man, epideictic as a compliment to parents of a beautiful baby, or ecphrastic of a painting or statue of a youth. The conceit was later borrowed twice by Meleager (for one of these poems, see epigram X in chapter 8).

XX (GP 16, AP 12.50)

A consolation poem addressed to the poet by a drinking companion. It was conventional even for the Greeks to say to a lover that he was not the only one who had ever fallen in love. Wine was usually diluted with water, so to drink "Bacchus straight" was a sign of serious imbibing. Moreover, the narrator of the poem is urging Asclepiades not to wait for sundown but to start the drinking early. Athenaeus in *Scholars at Dinner* quotes a poem of the Greek lyric poet Alcaeus from the late seventh or early sixth century BCE that says in part, "Let us drink! Why do we wait for the lamps? There is but a finger-length of day." Asclepiades borrows this expression, though in typical Hellenistic fashion he uses a different Greek word for "day," one that usually means "dawn," and this has confused many commentators. The word for "lamp" is modified with the adjective *koimistes,* which means "putting to bed" or "bedtime," as I have translated it. I have placed this poem last, since, as Gutzwiller has observed in *Poetic Garlands,* the poet's name in the first line may have served as a *sphragis,* or "seal"—in effect, the poet's signature, sometimes found near the beginning or end of a Greek book. The subject of the poem also seems fitting to end a poetry collection, since "night" and "death" were often used then as now as words of closure.

CHAPTER FIVE

Posidippus

Posidippus was born perhaps twenty years after Asclepiades in the city of
Pella, the capital of Macedonia and the birthplace of Alexander the
Great. Some of Posidippus's poems can be dated from their subject mat-
ter and show that he was active at least from 284 BCE to 250 BCE, the
period of the greatest flowering of Hellenistic literature. During much of
this time he wrote epigrams in honor of his rulers and other prominent
figures in the Ptolemaic kingdom, so he is likely to have spent a large part
of his life in Alexandria associated with the court. Surviving inscriptions
show that he was given the honorific title of *proxenos* (foreign representa-

tive) at Delphi about 276–272 BCE, and again at Thermon ten years later, presumably for services rendered. The inscription at Thermon refers to him as an *epigrammatopoios,* or a professional composer of epigrams. In one of his poems, written when he was an old man, he addresses his native Pella and asks that he still be held dear to his city and that his house and wealth be left to his children. The picture we have, then, is of a poet coming of age in the capital city of Macedonia on mainland Greece, leaving as a young man for Alexandria and establishing himself there as a court poet in association with the Ptolemies, occasionally traveling back to Greece to write epigrams (perhaps in some official capacity), and eventually returning to Pella, where at some point during his life he had acquired a family with wife and children. We do not know when he died.

Until quite recently, our view of Posidippus's poetry was highly colored by the selection of poems Meleager included in his *Garland* (see chapter 1). Our understanding of Posidippus's work has changed considerably as the result of the discovery and publication of the Milan papyrus, a scroll from an Egyptian mummy containing an additional 112 epigrams. Sometime in the second century BCE, an embalmer was making a mummy using cartonnage—that is, layers of linen or, in this case, papyrus stuck together to make a shell coated with plaster. The papyrus employed for the chest piece of the mummy contained a discarded collection of poems. This particular mummy was later buried near the Egyptian town of Fayum (now Al Fayyum), southwest of Cairo. After being unearthed probably by grave diggers, it passed through several hands, making its way to Europe. It was eventually purchased in the late 1990s on behalf of the University of Milan with funds from the Italian bank Cariplo.

Once extracted from the rest of the mummy, the papyrus was found to consist of a book of poetry without its beginning or end and without any title or indication of authorship. The great majority if not all of the epigrams are quite likely by the same author, since they display clear consistencies of style and theme; and fortunately, two of them had been previously attributed to Posidippus. That Posidippus wrote the poems of the Milan papyrus is now widely accepted by nearly all of the scholars who have studied them. A few have objected that the quality of the poetry is uneven, and that some of the verse is too poorly written to be the work of the same author who wrote the love poems collected by Meleager. But all collections of poetry, even by the greatest poets, are uneven, and Meleager may have taken many of the best poems. Even if Posidippus did not write all the epigrams in the Milan papyrus, these poems were clearly written during the Hellenistic period and are just as worthy of our attention as any of the other poetry in this volume.

If the poems in the Milan papyrus are by Posidippus, we must significantly modify our view of his interests and range as a poet. Only one or perhaps two epitaphs by Posidippus had been collected in the *Greek Anthology,* but epitaphs of one kind or another constitute the most numerous category of poems in the Milan papyrus. Most of these poems were written for women and bear a striking resemblance to the epitaphs of Anyte and of Leonidas of Tarentum. There are also many poems about stones, particularly gemstones. We knew previously of one poem like this by Posidippus about a snake stone (XIX), but the Milan papyrus gives us this poem and nineteen more (see XVII–XXI). Another category of epigram, about victories in horse races (for example, XV and XVI), is familiar to us from actual inscriptions (see the introduction to chapter 10) but had not been previously attested among poets of the Hellenistic era. Yet another category contains the only Hellenistic epigrams we have on prophecy, particularly from the flight and cry of birds (XXII–XXVI). In addition, there are poems in the Milan papyrus in the form of dedications that are panegyrics addressed mainly to Arsinoe II, sister and wife of Ptolemy II (for example, XIII). Before the discovery of the Milan papyrus, praise epigrams were so rare among Hellenistic poets that many scholars had thought these poets were disinclined to write them, though there is ample evidence for panegyric poetry during the Hellenistic era in longer verse forms. The Milan papyrus also includes seven poems on miraculous cures (see XXVII–XXX), clearly based on tablets and inscriptions set up at major Greek shrines for the god of medicine Asclepius; such epigrams, too, had been so rare among Hellenistic poets that their appearance in the Milan papyrus in a separate section came as a complete surprise.

We had previously thought of Posidippus as mainly a love poet, but the Milan papyrus contains no love epigrams. Since we do not have all of the scroll from which the Milan papyrus was taken and may even have as little as half of it, it is possible that love poems were gathered in the portion now lost. The discovery of the Milan papyrus has demonstrated that at least one Hellenistic poet wrote epigrams on a very wide range of topics, and if this was true of Posidippus, it may have been true of many of the other poets as well.

I

Now Pella and the maenads thrice lament
Nikó, the youngest child of twelve, who went
As Bacchic servant to the mystic rites;
Fate brought her back down from the mountain heights.

II

I'm old Batís. Athenodíkë hired
Me here in Phókaia, I was required
To toil at spinning for my daily wage.
I lived among small children to great age,
Instructing how to work the wool and thread
To plait the hairnets girls put round their head,
And colored headbands that they tie below.
But these young maidens, now about to go
Up to the threshold of their bridal room,
Have put me, old "cane-bearer," in my tomb.

III

    Oh passerby, see: Timon stays
Now buried underground, just over there;
    But this sundial to part the days
He built, and left this maiden for its care.
    However much hope can foresee,
The maid will read time, till her time is done.
    To you, long life! In long years, she
By this stone measures out the lovely sun.

IV

Why, sailors, do you bury me near the sea?
Much further off Nikétes' tomb should be.
I shudder at the echo of the wave,
Which wrecked my ship, and this fate to me gave.
But since you've pitied me, I've this to say:
Farewell! And for your help, thanks anyway.

V

Why have you stopped, won't let me sleep,
And, standing near my gravestone, keep
On asking from what land I came,
And who's my father, what's my name?
Go past my marker! I am one
Menoítios from Crete, the son
Of Phílarchos. That's it, get walking!
We foreigners don't like much talking.

VI

You don't ask where, from whom, or who
I am, as you're supposed to do,
But pass on by. Come look, and see
Sosés here lying peacefully,
Alkaíos was my father's name,
My country's Kos, like yours, the same.

VII

Don't think your specious tears lead me astray.
I know: for though you, Philainís, may say
When you're with me, your love for none is greater,
To someone else you'd say the same thing later.

VIII

If Pythiás is busy, I won't stay;
But if she sleeps alone, bring me inside.
Give her this message: drunk, I made my way
Through thieves, with reckless Eros as my guide.

IX

Oh tears and revels, why do you conspire
To stir the embers of another yearning,
Before my feet are lifted from the fire?
I can't stop loving; always undiscerning,
And fraught with some new pain, is my desire.

X

Yes Cupids, yes! Come shoot me, have your fun!
There's lots of you, of me there's only one!

Don't spare me, fools. Deliver!
For if I'm overthrown,
As famous master-archers you'll be known
Among the gods, from the volume of your quiver.

XI

In thorns lies the cicada of the Muses;
For Póthos, god of love's desire,
Imprisons him, pelts him with fire
Beneath the ribs, and hopes that this reduces

His song to slumber. But past application
Of his soul to his books now reaps
A different harvest, and he heaps
Upon the pesky god his castigation.

XII

Well-armed I'll fight you, Eros, and although
A mortal, I'll not flinch! So drop your bow!
If you would catch me drunk, then usher me
Off to captivity;
But if I'm in my senses,
I shall have reason bracing my defenses.

XIII

This fillet, Arsinóë, is for you,
Fine linen cloth whose pleats the wind blows through,
From Naúkratis. For once a maiden dreamed
You wished to wipe sweet sweat off, when you seemed
To pause from busy labor and stand near,
Shield on your arm and, in your hand, sharp spear.
That Macedonian maid at your command,
Called Hegesó, gave, Mistress, this white band.

XIV

This bronze by Hekataíos was so made
True to Philítas, to the tips of his toes,
That in its height and body, he's portrayed
In human measure, and the sculpture shows
No trace of the heroic, but is wrought
With utmost skill, so to the truth adhering
By such straight rule, that he seems lost in thought
Over some gloss, the old man, and appearing
Almost to speak. So finely worked is he,
With so much character elaborated,
That full of life the elder looks to be,
Though bronze: "A man from Kos, I'm dedicated
Here to the Muses, who teach us to sing,
By order of Ptolemy, god and king."

XV

A filly once in Delphi was competing
As trace horse of a chariot, and beating
(Though neck and neck) the others by a nose,
A great cry from the charioteers arose,
Much shouting right beside the referees,
Men chosen from the nationalities
Of all of Greece. The judges then threw down
Their rods, to signal that the victory crown
Should be assigned by lot, but with a nod,
That right-hand trace horse gathered up a rod,
Brave girl with simple heart among the guys!

Then all the people shouted that the prize
Should go to her, and so to great acclaim,
The chariot owner Kallikrátes came
To take the laurel. This bronze of the race,
So lifelike it could almost take its place,
With horses, chariot, and charioteer,
To Sibling Gods that Samian man placed here.

XVI

As kings, the first and only three
In chariots at Olympia, we,
Myself and my two parents, won.
Here's me, the one unpaired, the son
Of Bereníkě, with the name
Of Ptolemy, which is the same
As Father's, and my family
Is Eördaían; here with me,
These two, my parents. I don't rate
My father's glory as so great,
But Mother, though a woman, beat
The other horses—what a feat!

XVII

Timánthes carved a Persian half-stone gem
     Of lapus lazuli, and sold
This piece with starlike flecks of gold
     Then to Demýlos. Next from him,
Dark-haired Nikaía got it, and for this
     She traded him a tender kiss.

XVIII

A winter river rolling yellow threw
Down from Arabian mountains to the sea
This gemstone of a honey-colored hue,
Carved by the hand of Krónios. Now free
To wander on its necklace hanging low,
Inlaid and bound in gold, it's come to rest,
A honeyed brilliance shining in the glow
Upon the white of Nikonóë's breast.

XIX

No river rumbling in its banks, instead
    A bearded snake head
Once bore this gem with ample streaks of white.
    Lýnkeian eyesight
Engraved on it a chariot, as fine
    As a mark or line
On a fingernail, incised, with no part raised.
    You would be amazed
A jeweler could carve this, without impairing
    His eyes from staring.

XX

Down to the shore this crystal rock of gray
Was tossed along by an Arabian stream,
Forever tearing from the hills away
Great clods of earth. That's why it does not seem
To foolish men like gold: were there just one
Or two rocks made like this, we would esteem
Its splendor like the beauty of the sun.

XXI

See what Olympus from its height
Has rooted up, this stone of double might:
   Just like a magnet in one place,
It easily draws iron face-to-face;
   But in another, now the stone
Repels, the opposite. All on its own,
   How wonderful what it can do!
This one elongate rock can mimic two!

XXII

To see in the morning shearwaters diving low
Down to the ocean's breakers, is to know
   The auguries are good,
   And, fisherman, you should
Cast hook, throw net and traps, and without fail,
When you go home you'll have no empty pail.

XXIII

If at a crossroads, someone takes the way
   To baneful battle, while perceiving
   An old man weeping, then he's leaving
Never to see home again. Let him delay

His journey for some later strife. We mourn
   The Phocian Timoléon, who
   Came back with all his fighting through,
And who had heaped this prophecy with scorn.

XXIV

If in a single place, someone would see
Both larks and finches, hatred is foreshown;
Together they mean danger lies ahead.
Euélthon saw them once like this, when he
Was walking as a traveler alone:
Cruel robbers in Sidénë struck him dead.

XXV

When on a wooden image sweat appears,
What grief to townsmen, what snowstorm of spears
    Is hastening its way!
    But to this same god pray,
And, sweating, he will drive the flames of woe
Back to the homes and harvests of the foe.

XXVI

From this hill, with its panoramic view,
Can Damon of good parentage deduce
Your fate from flights of birds. So come! And you
Will learn the auguries and word of Zeus.

XXVII

On crutches Anticháres, lame,
        Trailing his feet,
To you, Asclepius, once came
        By the shortest street;
And when he'd sacrificed to you,
        Though long in bed,
He stood on both his legs anew,
        And fled.

XXVIII

A silver bowl, Asclepius, as gift
    For his recovery, to show
His thanks to you, Sosés of Kos imparted,
Whose sacred sickness you arrived to lift
    Away, with his six years of woe,
All in one night, oh god; then you departed.

XXIX

Asclás from Crete was deaf, and didn't know
The clash of waves or clattering of squalls,
Prayed to Asclepius, then left to go
Straight home, to hear talk even through brick walls.

XXX

When Zenon should have slept a quiet sleep,
For twenty-five years blind, and in his eighties,
He suddenly was cured, but could just keep
His sight two days, before he saw cruel Hades.

EXPLANATORY NOTES

I (AB 44)

The majority of the epitaphs in the Milan papyrus are for women, especially for young girls who died before marriage. This particular example is significant for two reasons: the girl was from Pella, where Posidippus was born and probably had family and owned property, and she was a maenad—that is, an adept of the Bacchic mystery rites. She apparently died while participating in a bacchanalian ritual, of whose exact nature we cannot be sure but which may have involved drunkenness and energetic dancing. She was carried back down from the mountains, where the rites of Dionysus were normally celebrated. Since she was lamented by the entire city of Pella, her family likely was wealthy. We know that there was an active cult of Dionysian mystery religion at Pella, since it is the site of ancient graves, dating probably from the end of the fourth century BCE, that contain small gold lamellae in the shape of laurel or myrtle leaves. These lamellae, imprinted with the names of initiates, are known to have been placed in the mouth or on the chest of the corpse. One of these lamellae says: "to Persephone, Posidippus, a pious initiate" and was intended to instruct Persephone, the goddess of the underworld, to direct the bearer Posidippus to the resting place of the blessed. The lamella is in a grave too old to have been made for the poet Posidippus, but it may have belonged to his grandfather or other relative. For Posidippus to have been initiated would be unsurprising and indeed seems likely, given the text of a longer elegiac poem that has come down to us on two wax tablets discovered in Egypt. In this work, called the "Seal of Posidippus," the poet names himself as Posidippus, gives his home town as Pella, and asks that a statue be placed in the city showing him about to unroll a poetry book, presumably to read his poems to his countrymen. He also asks in old age to travel "the mystic path to Rhadamanthus," one of the judges of the underworld—a journey permitted only to those who had undergone initiation. The evidence, though not incontrovertible, seems on the whole rather strong that the author of this poem is the same Posidippus who wrote the epigrams of the Milan papyrus.

II (AB 46)

In addition to those about young girls, several epitaphs describe elderly women who died after long and productive lives. This poem, like Leonidas V, is about a *chernetis,* a destitute woman who spun for a daily wage. Batis also looked after infants and young girls in the household and taught spinning. She must have been a beloved taskmaster, since the girls gave her a proper burial with a tombstone (not usually accorded a poor woman). The poem refers to Batis in its last line as a *narthekophoros,* a bearer of a *narthex.* The word *narthex* can mean a schoolmaster's cane, which Batis may have used to keep the children in line; but this word can also refer to a stalk of giant fennel, wreathed at its top with leaves and a pine cone, which was carried by devotees of Dionysus. Posidippus may be hinting that Batis was herself an initiate and may have had the additional role of helping the girls participate in the mystery rites.

III (AB 52)

This poem for the man Timon is surrounded in the Milan papyrus by epitaphs for young girls and seems out of place. Its focus, however, is on a sundial placed in a cemetery not far from a grave, and on the girl whom Timon "left" for its care. Our initial expectation is that this young maiden is one of Timon's children left behind when Timon died, since many Greek epitaphs refer to children "left" by dying parents, and Posidippus uses the same verb—*leipo*—found in many actual inscriptions in the tense normally employed. The poem plays with this meaning, saying that the maiden will continue to read the hours for as long as we can have any hope of her doing so, as would a mortal consulting the sundial until her death. It is, however, more than likely that the maid of the poem was meant to be a supporting stone or column in the shape of a young woman, called a caryatid. Greek sundials were viewed from below rather than from above and thus were placed on a column of some kind; there are several surviving examples of sundials supported by caryatids. The image of the girl on the caryatid may have been looking upward at the sundial, reading time "till her time is done," when she would fall to decay with the rest of the cemetery.

IV (AB 132, GP 15, AP 7.267)

Though the Milan papyrus contains six epigrams in a section entitled *nauagika,* or "shipwrecked," this epitaph for a shipwrecked man is not among them and comes to us from Meleager's *Garland.* This discrepancy is of some interest, since it would seem to indicate that the Milan papyrus may not have been a complete edition of Posidippus's poems. The ship-wrecked man Niketes in the epigram complains that his grave is placed too close to the sea, but he grudgingly thanks the sailors who buried him for their well-meaning intentions. Posidippus's epigram may have been influenced by Asclepiades I on a similar theme.

V and VI (AB 102 and 103)

These two poems are from a section of the Milan papyrus called *tropoi*, which can mean "characters" or "habits" as well as "manners" or "fashions." All eight epigrams in this section are epitaphs, and these first two, which are the best preserved, present attitudes of men of diametrically opposed characters. In both poems the deceased men address the passerby and refer explicitly to information usually provided on the tombstone: the name of the deceased, together with his or her patronymic and land of origin. In the first the dead man is from Crete and a foreigner; in the second he is from Kos and apparently buried in his hometown, since he refers to the passerby as having the same nationality. The first poem plays on the reputation of Cretans in antiquity as men of few words. The buried man in the second is Soses, a name we shall encounter again in XXVIII.

VII (AB 125, GP 2, AP 5.186)

The following six poems of Posidippus are love epigrams that have come to us from Meleager's *Garland*. They are all connected in some way to poems of Asclepiades, mirroring his themes or presenting contrasting points of view on similar subjects. The Philainis of this poem reminds us of winsome Hermione of Asclepiades XVIII. Both women are courtesans, or at least women with more than one lover. In Asclepiades' poem, Hermione explicitly reveals her promiscuity in the embroidery on her *zonion* and asks her various lovers to accept the situation and not be angry with her. What makes that epigram amusing is the woman's open confession of what her lovers would suspect in any case. In Posidippus's poem, in contrast, the poet is clearly angry with Philainis, who is *not* confessing and tries to deceive him with tears. Posidippus's poem is cleverly written but more conventional in its treatment than Asclepiades XVIII.

VIII (AB 130, GP 4, AP 5.213)

This poem has clear affinities with Asclepiades XI (see chapter 1). In Asclepiades the poet is outraged that the girl won't open her door even though he claims to have been invited. In Posidippus the poet has not been invited, at least not yet, and his attitude toward the servant at the door is more matter-of-fact. The message he gives, that he made his way drunk and through thieves with Eros as his guide, is intended to convince Pythias of his passion; but it seems—to us, if not to the girl—a bit glib.

IX (AB 129, GP 3, AP 5.211)

The reference in this poem to the never-ceasing urgency of love reminds us of Asclepiades VI, and the moral is much the same: why do I go from one affair to the next and never have any release from sexual desire? The themes of Asclepiades VII and XX are also similar. Posidippus uses fire and embers as metaphors of desire, as does Asclepiades (see VI, VII, XVII, and XX). Posidippus calls his desire "undiscerning," in Greek literally "not choosing or deciding"; in Asclepiades VI, the Cupids continue to play knucklebones in supreme indifference to the fate of their victims.

X (AB 135, GP 5, AP 12.45)

This poem is also adapted from Asclepiades. Posidippus calls the gods of desire the *Erotes* or "Cupids," in the plural here as also in Asclepiades VI and VII. The phrase *nai nai ballete, Erotes*—literally, "Yes, yes, strike me, Cupids"—is repeated in this poem word for word from Asclepiades VII. Asclepiades VI refers to the Cupids as *aphrones,* "lacking judgment," which I there translated "heedless." In the poem of Posidippus, this same word is used as a noun and has a meaning closer to "fools." In Asclepiades VII the poet invites the gods to destroy him, if not with arrows then with thunderbolts. The mood in Posidippus X is rather different. The poet says defiantly that the Cupids may overcome him, but doing so will require so many arrows that the Cupids will be famous ever after for the great capacity of the quiver each manages to carry about. The impression given us by this poem and by many of the rest of his love epigrams is that Posidippus as the younger poet was reacting to and varying the themes and phrasing of Asclepiades, whose work served as his most important model.

XI (AB 137, GP 6, AP 12.98)

Cicadas are large, winged insects whose males sing a loud mating call. By analogy, "the cicada of the Muses" is a poet who sings his verse. This cicada has been imprisoned in thorns by Pothos, the god of longing and sexual desire. The ancient Greeks thought that the cicadas of Acanthus (a coastal city in the north of Greece) couldn't sing, and *akantha* in Greek means "thorn" or "thistle." By placing the poet among thorns, the god has therefore effectively turned him into a mute cicada unable to sing poetry, and Pothos fills the poet's heart with sexual passion in an attempt to reduce him to silence. But the poet is defiant. Having spent many years laboring among books, he has steeled his soul against the distractions of lust (or at least he says he has) and heaps upon the god his reproaches.

XII (AB 138, GP 7, AP 12.120)

This is the last of the love poems I have selected, and it continues the themes of the preceding two. The poet is well-armed against desire, presumably from his scholarly study of philosophy, and he calls upon Eros to drop his bow. His rebellion is qualified in the rest of the poem by his admission that if drunk, he will offer no resistance, though if sober, he will have reason as a defense against desire. This is an odd stance for a poet of amorous verse; much more typical is the attitude displayed in Asclepiades XX, where a friend urges the poet to drink to forget about his unhappy love affair. We can of course have no idea whether Posidippus wrote this poem because he really believed his learning could preserve him from a life of capricious infatuation, or whether he was consciously attempting to take an unconventional stance, thereby following the Hellenistic tradition of inverting the commonplace and varying the topics of other poets.

XIII (AB 36)

The Milan papyrus has a section containing six dedication epigrams; four are addressed to Queen Arsinoe II, sister and wife of Ptolemy II Philadelphus, king of Egypt from 282 BCE to 246 BCE. These poems are among the many epigrams Posidippus wrote with political themes or in eulogy of his rulers, who were Macedonian Greeks and therefore Posidippus's fellow countrymen. A fillet is a strip of cloth tied around the brow of the head. As a symbol of royalty, Greek kings and queens (including Alexander the Great) wore a strip of cloth around the head called a *diadema,* or "diadem," whose ends were left free to hang down in the back. The fillet that Hegeso dedicates may be intended to resemble such a cloth. It was made in Naucratis, an important Greek trading center on the Nile first established under the pharaohs. The maiden Hegeso has dreamed that Arsinoe was laboring in battle, perhaps in support of the Egyptian army, and has asked for a cloth to wipe the queen's sweat away. Arsinoe and her brother were deified in 272/271 BCE and were worshipped in temples throughout Egypt, where the dedication may have been made. The poem was probably written after Arsinoe's death, since a spirit would more appropriately appear in a dream than would a person still alive. Arsinoe is represented as wearing a shield and holding a spear. Macedonian queens had a long tradition of wearing armor, and some are thought even to have fought in battle.

XIV (AB 63)

This is perhaps the most interesting of the nine poems on bronze statues contained in the Milan papyrus. Epigrams written to describe or accompany works of art were composed by Anyte (XII, XIII), Leonidas (XXIV), Theocritus (XII), and many other Hellenistic poets. What makes this poem by Posidippus different is that it not only describes the statue, it also presents a philosophy of aesthetics compatible with much of Hellenistic art. For just as Hellenistic poets generally avoided a grand manner and heroic style, emphasizing smaller genres and precision of phrasing, so the visual artists attempted to portray nature as accurately as possible, with a realism they opposed to the heroic idealism of Polycleitus, Phidias, and other earlier Greek sculptors. Little is known about Hekataios. He is mentioned by Pliny the Elder as an engraver of silver, but nothing is known about his statues. Philitas, the subject of the statue, was famous in antiquity as an Homeric scholar and poet, whose verse is mentioned not only by the Greeks but also by Propertius and Ovid, though almost none of it has survived. Philitas was the tutor of Ptolemy II and was known in antiquity for his exacting study of obscure words in Greek epic and also for his thinness; he is jokingly said to have worn lead in his shoes to avoid being blown away in a strong wind. There is uncertainty about the wording at the end of the poem, and I have followed the suggestion of Michael Haslam and Ruth Scodel that the statue actually speaks (see Scodel's article). The Ptolemy in the poem who was both god and king is Ptolemy II Philadelphus (see note to XIII).

XV (AB 74)

The Milan papyrus contains eighteen poems in a section entitled *hippika,* or horse race epigrams. Although only a few epigrams of this type were transmitted by Hellenistic poets in Meleager's *Garland,* Pindar's *Odes* celebrated chariot victories, as did many inscriptions on stone that still survive. The winning of a chariot victory was as important in ancient Greece as an Olympic victory today—perhaps even more important, since the winners were often political figures eager to advertise their personal power. Just as now at the Kentucky Derby, the winner at Delphi or Olympus was not the chariot driver or the trainer (though they are sometimes mentioned in commemorative poetry) but the owner, the one who paid the bills—in this poem Kallikrates of Samos, who was commander of the navy and a close associate of the Ptolemies. Thus this poem is not simply a vivid description of a chariot race but also a panegyric epigram in honor of Kallikrates; in addition, as its ending makes clear, it is a description of a bronze statue, like the preceding poem. Greek chariots were drawn by two horses attached to a central pole, but an additional two horses could be added abreast, fastened on either side of the central pair by a bar or rope called a "trace" that was connected to the front of the chariot. The strongest horses were placed in the center, but the trace horses are often shown slightly in the lead. The judges at Delphi are called "Amphictyonic" by Posidippus, a reference to the Amphictyonic League whose representatives—originally drawn from twelve of the tribes of Greece—met to maintain temples and mediate regional disputes. The officials of the Amphictyonic League organized the Pythian Games at Delphi, where this chariot race took place. The statue of the chariot is called in the poem *enarges,* "manifest to the eye" or "lifelike," and so had many of the same virtues Posidippus admired in the statue of Philitas in epigram XIV. The Sibling Gods to whom the statue is dedicated are Arsinoe II and Ptolemy Philadelphus, and the Samian man is Kallikrates.

XVI (AB 88)

This poem, like the preceding, is a panegyric; it probably describes a statue of a family grouping representing Ptolemy II (the voice of the poem) and his two parents, Ptolemy I Soter and Berenike I. All three were victorious in chariot racing at Olympia. This poem is one of several of the *hippika* in the Milan papyrus that mention the victory of Berenike I, who was one of very few women ever to win at chariot racing. She was not, however, the first—that distinction apparently went to Kyniska from the royal family of Sparta more than a hundred years earlier. A surviving inscription (Ebert 33, *AP* 13.16) says,

> My fathers and brothers are Spartan kings, and I,
> Kyníska, with fleet chariot have won.
> I put my statue here to testify
> That of Greek women I'm the only one.

Women were not even allowed to enter Olympia during the games, though this did not prevent Kyniska or later Berenike I from being represented there by a chariot and driver. Eordaia is the province in the western part of Macedonia from which the Ptolemies originally came. The reading of the Milan papyrus is unclear near the poem's end, and in particular it is not certain exactly what Ptolemy II says about his father. The reading I have chosen is only one among several possibilities but is, I think, the most interesting.

XVII (AB 5)

One of the great surprises of the Milan papyrus was the discovery of a long section containing poems about stones, particularly gemstones. Only a very few epigrams like this from Hellenistic poets had been previously known. This poem is about a piece of jewelry of lapis lazuli, a deep-blue semiprecious stone with golden flecks of pyrite that was popular in Egypt and throughout the Middle East; the best-quality lapis lazuli was mined then (as now) in Afghanistan, perhaps the Persia referred to in the poem. It is unclear what Posidippus meant by "half-stone." This is one of several of Posidippus's poems on gems that double as love epigrams.

XVIII (AB 7)

The origin of the stone is again exotic, this time Arabia; it is yellow but cannot otherwise be identified. Kronios is an historical figure, a well-known Hellenistic gem carver. The gem was mounted (probably as the centerpiece) on a necklace called a *kathema,* which was a pendent necklace long enough to descend all the way to the breasts. The stone would have been visible only if worn outside the garment or (as here) in décolletage.

XIX (AB 15, GP 20)

This is one of only two poems in the Milan papyrus previously ascribed to Posidippus, known not from Meleager's *Garland* but from the *Chiliades* or *Book of Histories* of the twelfth-century Byzantine scholar John Tzetzes. Snakes are often described as "bearded" in antiquity, though it is unclear how this myth arose. There are several Greek and Latin reports (now known to be erroneous) of a whitish, transparent stone, found in the brain tissue of a snake but only if the snake was still alive. Pliny the Elder says in his *Natural History* that this stone could be collected by scattering sleeping drugs in front of a snake so that its head could be cut off before it died. Pliny also declares that stones from snake brains could not be carved, though this was clearly not the case for the stone of this epigram. "Lynkeian" eyesight is the eyesight of Lynkeus, who was proverbial for his keen vision during the voyage of the *Argo,* the ship Jason sailed in search of the golden fleece.

XX (AB 16)

In XVIII, a winter river rolls down a yellow gemstone from the Arabian mountains, and in XIX, the poet is careful to say that "no river rumbling in its banks" bore the stone but rather the head of a snake. Here we are drawn back to Arabia, though what is "tossed along by an Arabian stream" turns out to be not a gemstone but rather a lovely rock of crystal much like a polished beach pebble, of much beauty but no value. These stone poems, all from the Milan papyrus, show the poet carefully varying his themes in a way that is typically Hellenistic, so that the poems are interrelated not just by their similarities but also by their differences.

XXI (AB 17)

Another rock that is not a gemstone, thrown down not from Arabian mountains but rather from Mount Olympus. The Olympus in question is not the familiar Greek home to the gods but Mysian Olympus—now called Uludag and located in Bursa Province in the northwest of Turkey. The rock is a magnet and has a property rare in antiquity of having distinct north and south poles, so that one side of the rock can attract iron and the other repel it. Although magnets were known to the Greeks and Romans, and both attraction and repulsion are recorded (by Lucretius, for example), the written record contains no recognition that both can be produced—as here—by opposite sides of the same rock. The first mention of such a phenomenon (at least before the discovery of this poem) dates to the fifth century CE. This property is what makes the rock of the poem so precious and unusual. The reading of the last line of the poem is disputed. I have translated *probolos,* which usually means "projecting," in the nominative as "elongate," since a rock having distinct north and south poles would have to be of this shape in order for its two poles to be sufficiently far apart.

XXII (AB 23)

The next five epigrams that I have selected are from a section of the Milan papyrus about prophecy. A few epigrams like this were transmitted in the *Greek Anthology,* but the Milan papyrus gives us a far larger sample from a single poet than was previously available. Mediterranean shearwaters are seabirds of the genus *Puffinus,* which feed on small fish and squid. They dive down into the water from the air, entering at an angle of about 45 degrees in an awkward-looking belly flop from a height of generally no more than 3–5 meters. They then swim quite efficiently under water to catch their prey. This poem is surrounded by others about prophecy from the flight of birds (see note to XXVI below), but it is really a poem about the weather (diving shearwaters were thought by the Greeks to foretell rain), conveying not much more than fisherman's lore. It would take little knowledge of soothsaying to conclude from the active feeding of seabirds that fish are likely to be in the vicinity.

XXIII (AB 28)

In this epigram, an old man weeping at a crossroads is an omen of death in battle. Timoleon, who is not otherwise known, apparently saw this portent as he was departing for war and made fun of it. He is given as a supportive example of the omen's truth, since he returned from the fighting as an object of mourning—that is, as a corpse. There is an interesting ambiguity at the beginning of the poem, since the Greek word for an elder or old man, *presbys* (as in Presbyterian), can also mean "wren." Accordingly, David Petrain has argued that the omen is not about a weeping old man but rather a wailing wren. An old man seems nevertheless to make better sense thematically, since fathers weeping for sons slain in battle are a conventional feature of Greek literature at least from the time of Priam and Hector. That is not to say, however, that we should simply ignore the meaning "wren," since it is quite possible that Posidippus intentionally used *presbys* because of its double meaning.

XXIV (AB 29)

Many examples of birds and other animals thought by the Greeks to be naturally antagonistic to one another are given in Aristotle's *Historia Animalium*. Because of the supposed enmity of larks and finches, their presence together in one place was taken to be an unfavorable omen. The name Euelthon means "well-traveling" and was probably invented by the poet as ironic commentary on the man's sorry ending. Sidene was a city south of Troy on the northwestern coast of what is now Turkey.

XXV (AB 30)

Sweating statues as portents of disaster are often mentioned in Greek and Latin literature. Plutarch says that Alexander the Great, as he was embarking on his eastern campaign, saw a wooden statue of Orpheus sweating. This omen caused much apprehension but was interpreted favorably by one of Alexander's followers to mean that Alexander would cause much toil to poets celebrating his victories. In the event, the campaign was a great success, though Alexander never returned to celebrate his victories.

XXVI (AB 34)

A sign or nameplate for a place of business (see also Theocritus IX). Few surviving signs have been discovered in Greek, though many have been found in Latin. One rare Hellenistic example from Memphis in Egypt reads, "I interpret dreams taking my orders from the god; here's good luck, this interpreter is from Crete." The second part of the inscription was apparently intended as reassurance to the customer, though why a Cretan interpreter of dreams would be better than any other isn't clear. Damon was an *oionistes,* or augur, who foretold the future from birds. The Greek and Roman practice of prophecy from birds probably came from the Near East. The *oionistes* claimed to be able to give personal and political counsel from the bird's manner of flying, its height, the sound and direction of its cry, and its placement in the sky, particularly of raptors such as eagles and hawks but also of wrens and herons. A hill with a "panoramic view" would be an optimal site for this practice.

XXVII (AB 96)

The last four poems of Posidippus that I have selected are again from
the Milan papyrus, from a section of epigrams describing sudden and
miraculous cures. Asclepius was the Greek god of medicine. In early
Greek literature (for example, Homer and Pindar), Asclepius was a hero
born of Apollo and a mortal mother and raised by the centaur Chiron.
He was so gifted in medicine that he was believed to be able to revive
the dead. At some point near the end of the sixth century BCE, Asclepius
began to be worshipped as a god, and a temple and altar were built for
him in the Greek city of Epidaurus. From there his worship spread and
temples to him were established all over the Greek world. By the time
of Posidippus, Asclepius was one of the most revered and honored of
Greek deities. Rich and poor alike thronged to his sanctuaries to seek
cures for illnesses; we know quite a lot about methods of treatment from
tablets and inscriptions left in Epidaurus and other centers of healing.
Patients were advised to sacrifice to the god, adopt special diets, imbibe
or apply drugs of one sort or another, swim or bathe in rivers or springs,
ride horses or take other physical exercise, and above all to sleep in a
building called an *abaton,* where the god would visit them during the
night in a process known as incubation. He would then either recom-
mend a remedy or effect an immediate cure. Many miraculous cures are
described in extensive collections of prose inscriptions that date from
the fourth century BCE and were originally placed like advertisements
on stone columns at Epidaurus, in full view of anyone who came to the
sanctuary. One of the inscriptions tells of a lame man sitting wide awake
in the temple as a boy came by and stole his crutch. The man immedi-
ately got up and ran after the boy, and so was cured. Inscriptions like
this at Epidaurus and other centers were undoubtedly the model for this
poem of Posidippus.

XXVIII *(AB 97)*

Since entry to a sanctuary of Asclepius was generally free, the dedications of bowls and other objects of value from grateful patients were an expected method of showing appreciation and providing payment for services rendered. Soses was apparently rich and could afford an expensive gift, but the temples were also willing to accept gifts of lesser value. In one of the surviving inscriptions at Epidaurus, Asclepius asked a boy what he could pay in return for his cure, and the boy answered "ten dice." The god laughed, took the dice, and cured him. The "sacred sickness" is epilepsy, which is said in the poem to have been cured "all in one night," presumably during an incubation.

XXIX *(AB 99)*

This poem seems to be a serious description of a miraculous cure of a deaf man until we get to the last line. The exaggerated claims in the inscriptions at the temples of Asclepius provided an easy target for a poet of epigrams.

XXX *(AB 100)*

The last poem I have selected was included in the Milan papyrus among the *iamatika* or "cure epigrams," but it has some features of an epitaph. The "quiet sleep" in the first line may refer to the sleep of death, which Zenon should have slept because he was so old. It could however also refer to incubation, which should have been "quiet"—that is to say, "undisturbed" by a visit from Asclepius—since even though Zenon was cured of his blindness, it did him little good because he died so soon afterward. The name "Hades" refers to the king of the underworld or the underworld itself, but the word in Greek is identical in spelling to the word meaning "unseen." The netherworld is, after all, hidden from view. So Zenon, who was blind, suddenly sees, then loses his sight and "sees" what is unseen.

CHAPTER SIX

Callimachus

Callimachus was the most famous and influential of all the Greek poets of the third century. His epigrams were read by schoolchildren, his poetry quoted and translated into Latin, and his name mentioned (usually with approval) in the verse of many of the most important Latin poets, including Catullus, Horace, Propertius, and Ovid. Since Callimachus used Asclepiades as a model in several of his epigrams, he probably belongs (like Posidippus) to the next generation of poets, born perhaps about 300 BCE. Callimachus came from the African city of Cyrene, originally a Greek colony but later a part of the empire of the Ptolemies in what is now Libya. Callimachus tells us (in epigram IV) that his grandfather was also named Callimachus and led the army of Cyrene; the poet's family is likely therefore to have been wealthy and part of the ruling class. He was a pupil of the grammarian Hermocrates and was appointed as a royal page to the court of the Ptolemies. According to the *Suda,* he married the daughter of Euphrates of Syracuse and lived during the reigns of both Ptolemy II Philadelphus and Ptolemy III Euergetes, dying perhaps about 240 BCE.

Though never actually the head of the library at Alexandria, Callimachus was an important scholar associated with the court and took on the task of composing the *Pinakes* or *Tablets,* a bibliographic encyclopedia in 120 scrolls of the books in the Alexandrian library. Surviving fragments of Callimachus's work show that it listed the books of each author with titles and often first lines, together with additional information of a biographical or literary nature. This must have been an enormous labor, since the books in the Alexandrian library included nearly all of the transmitted works of Greek literature. He is also said by the *Suda* to have written many additional scholarly books in prose, such as *On the Rivers in Europe, On Birds,* and *Names of Months According to Tribe and Cities.* Callimachus's great learning is on display in his poetry as well, especially in the fragments we have of his long elegiac poem the *Aitia* (or *Causes*), much of which consists of obscure explanations of minor religious customs or cultural traditions.

Other than his epigrams, the only poems of Callimachus that have survived nearly intact are the six *Hymns,* each 100–300 lines long; though different in structure from epigrams, they are of a style and character that reveal much about Callimachus the poet. The *Hymns* are modeled on the much older *Homeric Hymns,* which are based on myths of major gods and goddesses and may have been recited at religious festivals. Callimachus's poems seem superficially similar, but on closer reading they reveal themselves to be literary texts—witty, often irreverent, and sparkling with humor and learning. The first hymn, *To Zeus,* begins by asking what better god there could be for singing among libations, forever great, forever king; but it then ends by saying that no one could possibly praise all of Zeus's works, and it is the shortest of the hymns. *To Apollo* also seems to end abruptly, with Envy—symbolizing Callimachus's detractors—complaining about poets whose poems are too short, who don't "sing like the sea." Apollo (the god of poetry) then kicks Envy to one side and declares that "the Assyrian river is a great stream but carries lots of filth and rubbish" and that poetry should be "a small trickle, pure and undefiled from a holy spring." The fifth hymn, *On the Bath of Pallas,* is written in elegiac meter, an untraditional meter for a hymn though the most common meter for epigrams (see chapter 1); and the fifth and sixth hymns are both in an untraditional dialect. Callimachus used the form of an archaic hymn but took this genre into new territory, as if in exploration of the conventions upon which the genre was based.

He took much the same approach in his *Iambi,* which have survived only in fragments. The generic guidelines of iambic poetry were established by the work of two earlier Greek poets, Archilochus and Hipponax, who both used iambic meter to write satirical invective and personal slander. All of Callimachus's *Iambi* are also in some form of iambic meter, and Hipponax even appears in the first poem, a programmatic reminder of his importance for the genre. Callimachus then proceeded to write poems only marginally related to those of the earlier iambic poets, occasionally invective but usually not. There are poems with fables, several that explain obscure customs or sayings, three on statues, and one about a birthday celebration of a friend's daughter. Of the poems describing statues my favorite is the sixth, in which the poet gives a description of Phidias's statue of Zeus to a friend who is about to travel to Olympia. So far as we can tell from the fragments that remain, the poem says nothing about the beauty or charm of the statue, as would have been expected in a poem of this sort, but instead presents in verse a precise listing of each dimension of the statue and how much everything cost. In the thirteenth poem Callimachus is attacked by a critic for putting almost anything into his poetry, and he replies: "Who said, 'You there write elegiacs, you epic, but you were selected by the gods to write tragedy'? No one, I think."

Callimachus felt free to explore the boundaries of different genres and to mix one with another, inviting reproach but also providing an enormous stimulus to Greek literature and to his Latin imitators and followers.

This brings us to the *Epigrams*. These short poems, most of which have come to us from Meleager's *Garland,* are among the most accessible and widely appreciated of Callimachus's work. Much of the rest of his poetry makes for demanding reading, often bristling with obscure references and arcane vocabulary. Scholars began to write commentaries for the longer poems almost as soon as Callimachus died, and we still have some of these ancient "footnotes" or *scholia.* Callimachus had a reputation even among the ancients as a pedant, though the obscurities of his verse apparently did not prevent him from being appreciated by his contemporaries and by later Latin poets. The *Epigrams,* in contrast, contain a somewhat simpler vocabulary and are not so densely filled with recondite allusion. Some scholars think this indicates that they were written early in Callimachus's life, before his style had matured, but there is no evidence of this from the content of the poems and indeed some indication to the contrary. Callimachus probably wrote epigrams throughout his life but wrote them in a style unlike that of much of the remainder of his poetry.

Despite these differences from his other writings, the *Epigrams* nevertheless share many of the central concerns of Callimachus's art. Callimachus wrote a great many epitaphs and dedication epigrams, and some of these poems are so simple and so like actual inscriptions that it used to be thought that Callimachus made his living as a young man by writing inscribed verse for hire. A more likely explanation is that he intentionally provided in his collected poetry a spectrum of epitaphs and dedications, beginning with simple poems mimicking actual inscriptions and proceeding to poems of increasing complexity, which could never have been engraved on stone. As we saw in chapter 1, actual surviving inscriptions often address the reader passing by, telling him who is buried or to which god a gift is dedicated. Some of Callimachus's epigrams do this too, but in other poems it is the other way around: the passerby speaks to the deceased or the tomb, which may even answer back. These poems question the assumptions and limits of the genre much as the *Hymns* and *Iambi* do. In all of Callimachus's poetry, we learn to expect the unexpected and to take nothing at face value.

In addition to the epitaphs and dedications, Callimachus wrote many love epigrams. Like Posidippus, he was greatly influenced by Asclepiades, and their poems have many similarities of style and theme. There are nevertheless important differences. All but one of the surviving love poems that have been attributed to Callimachus are about boys, whereas both Asclepiades and Posidippus wrote mostly about women. Moreover, Callimachus was more likely to take a personal view, describing (or at least purporting to describe) his feelings about an affair of his own or of another person. Poems such as XXII, XXIV, XXV, and XXVII combine lighthearted sophistication with sensitivity and deep feeling in a way rarely found among the other third-century poets. For ancient love poetry with this same curious combination of disinterest and vulnerability, we have to look to the verse 200 years later of the Latin poet Catullus, a devoted admirer of Callimachus's work.

In addition to Catullus, who translated Callimachus and mentions him by name in his poetry, other Latin poets also expressed their appreciation. Propertius opens his third book of elegies by invoking the dead spirit of Callimachus at the beginning of a passage that rejects epic in favor of love elegy. Callimachus is probably mentioned here because he says in the prologue to the *Aitia* that he was criticized for not writing poetry "of kings and heroes," and so far as we know, he never wrote epic of the traditional kind. But what attracted Propertius and the other Latin poets to Callimachus may have been not so much the content of his poetry as its ethos. Callimachus argued on behalf of smaller genres, for poetry that is novel and original as well as highly polished, "pure and undefiled from a holy spring." The limited compass of an epigram is ideally suited to such a program.

Though the *Epigrams* are perhaps the most accessible of Callimachus's poems, they nevertheless often seem strange and enigmatic. Translations can give a misleading impression of simplicity and may fail to reveal the difficulties of interpretation posed by many of the poems. I have attempted to explain some of this complexity in the notes, but much of the allusiveness is as puzzling to scholars as to everyone else and makes Callimachus perhaps the most troublesome of the Hellenistic poets to translate satisfactorily. The translations I provide are as close as I can come to my understanding of the poems, and I hope that when read together with the notes, they give some appreciation for why Callimachus was so admired by his contemporaries and has continued to evoke so much interest and controversy among poets and scholars up to the present day.

I

The Samian daughters seek anew
    Their girlfriend best at play,
Krethís, of many stories, who
    Could chatter all the day;
But she, their sweetest helpmate, now
    Has gone to sleep below,
A slumber none can disavow,
    A debt that all girls owe.

II

Here Sáon son of Díkon's gone to lie
In sacred sleep. Don't say that good men die!

III

With all good things, when she was living still,
Míkkos took care of Aíschrë, "Good-Milk," till
She drew her last breath; then, to his nurse, he
Made this memorial for all to see
Who will come after, so he could attest
How much thanks that old girl got from her breast.

IV

Oh passerby, know this my grave
    Is sepulcher of one,
Who of Callimachus was both
    The father and the son;
And you must know them: one was once
    In battle our commander,
The other poetry composed
    Beyond the reach of slander.

V

You pass the tomb of Battiádes, who
    Splendidly knew
To sing, and in due measure could combine
    Laughter with wine.

VI

Is that Charídas under you? "Is he
Arímmas's son? If so, yes, under me."
Charídas, what's it like down there? "So black!"
And Pluto? "Myth!" Some way of coming back?
"A lie!" We're lost, there's nothing we can do!
"Well, all of this I've told you's really true,
But if it's something nice you want, they sell
A big ox for a penny here in Hell."

VII

Oh Timon, since you are no longer,
   Surely you can tell,
Is light or darkness worse? "The dark!
   There's more of you in Hell!"

VIII

Don't bless my grave, find something else to do.
I'm blessed enough, you shit. I'm rid of you!

IX

At dawn, we put Melánippos in his grave,
At sunset Basiló, his sister, gave
Her life away, because she could not bear
To live without her brother. Twofold care
Had their father Arístippos; Cyrénë grieved
To see him, blessed with children, now bereaved.

X

Who knows wherein the future, Charmis, lies,
Since you, but yesterday before our eyes,
Today we, weeping, to the graveyard bring?
Your father never saw a sadder thing.

XI

Who are you? Timonóë? Without name
Of father and the city whence you came
Here on the tombstone, I would not have known.
So sad must be your husband, all alone.

XII

Someone spoke, Heraclitus, of your fate,
    And that brought tears to me,
When I recalled how we two stayed up late
    So many times, how we

In talking made the sun go down. But though,
My friend from Halicarnassus, long ago

You must have been turned into ashes, still
    Your *Nightingales* will stay,
And Hades, plunderer of all things, will
    On them his hand not lay.

XIII

Menítas dedicates his bow
    And says this too: "I
Give, Sérapis, to you my horn
    And quiver; here's why
There are no arrows: they are with
    The Hesperítai."

XIV

Do come, Eileíthyia, to her yet again
    When Lykainís calls,
Helping in childbirth, easing her labor. Then
    May your perfumed halls,
Like this gift, Mistress, for a girl, enjoy
Another something later for a boy.

XV

The tub from which he took plain salt for bread,
And by his thrift great storms of debt has fled,
To Samothracian gods Eúdemos commended,
And "saved from the sea I give this, friends" appended.

XVI

Símos, son of Míkkos, gave
Me to the Muses, with a plea
For good marks, and like Glaúkos, they've
Bestowed this boon almost for free.
And here, a tragic mask, I lie
And gape wide open, twice as might
The Samian god. I'm Bacchus, I
Give ear to schoolboys who recite,
But they "my locks are sacred" say,
As if I'd never heard that play.

XVII

Euaínetos has dedicated me,
A bronze cock, in return for victory
   (At least he says it's so,
    I wouldn't really know)
To Castor and to Pollux, and I must
Place in the son of Phaidros all my trust.

XVIII

         He offered me to you,
    Oh Lion-Throttler, Slayer of the Swine,
       An oaken cudgel—"Who?"
Archínos. "Which?" From Crete. "It shall be mine."

XIX

This debt, Asclepius, you say to owe
Akéson praying for his woman, know
   Was not neglected;
   You collected.
If you forget, and your demand repeat,
This writing tablet shall be his receipt.

XX

A hunter, Epikýdes, through high peaks
Tracks every hare, of every deer he seeks
The footprints, though traversing frost and snow.
If someone says, "Look, here's a wounded doe,"
He does not take it. My love's like that too:
Whatever flees I know how to pursue,
But something that's already come to lie
In easy reach, I quickly pass on by.

XXI

I loathe a cyclic poem, nor can I bear
A road that carries many here and there;
   I also cannot stand
    A wandering lover, and
From such a spring I do not drink. I hate
Whatever's commonplace. "But you look great,
   Yes, Lysaníës, you
    Look great, you really do";
Before I can get out the final word,
An echo "someone's got him" first is heard.

XXII

Half of my soul's still living, but the rest,
Whether by Love or Hades now possessed,
I wouldn't know, except that it has fled.
Has it again gone to a boy? I said
So many times, "That runaway beware,
Don't take it, lads." Seek Theútimos, for there,
Fit to be stoned and sick in love, it's found
Some place, I know, where it can hang around.

XXIII

If dark Theocritus detests me, you
    May him four times more hate;
But if instead he loves me, oh then do
    To him reciprocate,
Olympian Zeus, by Ganymede I pray.
You too loved once. That's all I've got to say.

XXIV

But Ménippos, I know my purse is bare.
This is my own bad dream, and I despair
Each time I hear this bitter tale, from you
The most unloving thing that you could do.

XXV

If I caroused, Archínos, under no
    Constraint, then my behavior blame
    Ten thousand times, but if I came
Unwillingly, then let my rashness go.

For undiluted wine and Eros placed
    Me in their thrall, the one conveyed
    Me onward, and the other made
Me powerless to put aside my haste.

I've come but do not ask to be admitted;
    Giving no name, I placed a kiss
    Upon the doorpost, and if this
Is wrong, then wrong is what I have committed.

XXVI

There's something, by Pan, hidden, there's some fire
Beneath these ashes. Don't (I quake!) conspire
To catch me in your tangles! Streams that run
In silence have quite often walls undone
By gnawing unobserved. In this way now,
Menéxenos, I fear that you'll find how
To slip through my defenses, and can start
To steal without a sound into my heart.

XXVII

Kleónikos of Thessaly,
    By the bright sun I swear,
I didn't know you. Misery!
    You're now but bones and hair.

Where have you been? Or does the same
    God hold you who has me?
The same cruel fate? And is his name
    Euxitheós? I see:

You too like me are now his prize,
    Since, going to his place,
You looked, poor man, with both your eyes
    Full on his lovely face.

XXVIII

The guest kept his wound secret. Did you see?
The breath came from his chest so painfully;
By the third toast, the roses had all shed
Their petals to the floor down from his head.
His goose is cooked, and this is no surmise:
A thief, I know another thief's disguise.

XXIX

Orestes, lucky, yes, but crazy too,
Though not like me. I don't think that he knew
What happens when true friendship goes astray.
How could he, if he never wrote a play?
For if he had, he would have been like me,
With no Pyládes left for company.

XXX

A visitor asked Pittakós, the son
Of Hýrrhas, "Two young girls attract me, one
Is similar in wealth, dear sir, to me,
And with an equal birth and family,
The other is above me. So then, who's
The better? Tell me which one I should choose
To marry?" Then the old man raised his cane,
"See there," he said, "these children will explain
All that you need to know" (for over where
The elder pointed, boys in the broad square
Were spinning rapid tops), "Do as they do,"
He said, "and in their footsteps follow too."
The visitor approached and heard them say,
Each to his top, "Go keep to your own way,"
And hearing this gave up the greater bride,
Discerning what the boys had prophesied.
So you too, Díon, their precept obey,
Take home a poor wife, "keep to your own way."

EXPLANATORY NOTES

I (GP 37, AP 7.459, Pf 16)

Of the twelve poems that I have selected related to epitaphs, the first three most nearly resemble actual inscriptions. What makes this portrait of the girl Krethis so touching is the contrast between her garrulous animation and the finality of the grave, between the innocence of her companions who cannot stop searching for her and the cruelty of death in one so young. Callimachus's poem is so endearing that we are left wondering if Krethis was purely a product of his imagination or was based on a real girl. The poem says that Krethis is from the island of Samos, but Callimachus seems to have lived much of his life in Alexandria. The German scholar Wilamowitz therefore suggested that the girl's family may have belonged to a community of immigrants from Samos who had moved to Egypt. It is also possible that this poem is a variant of a lost epigram written by Asclepiades, who lived much of his life on Samos. There is ample evidence that Callimachus knew and varied the verse of Asclepiades, as we shall see in several of the love epigrams.

II (GP 41, AP 7.451, Pf 9)

This second epitaph also resembles many actual inscriptions. As in epigram I, death is represented as sleep—here, "sacred" sleep. It is unclear, however, why we are to say that good men don't die. Greeks who were initiated into mystery religions thought that good men lived after death in a kind of paradise, but such beliefs were not widespread (see epigram VI). Good men can, of course, also survive in the hearts and minds of those they leave after them. But another possibility is that we should read the last line as saying that if good men do not die and Saon is dead, he cannot have been a good man. Don't say good men die, say bad ones do! Most commentators have been inclined to read this poem as a simple attestation of the goodness of the deceased, as in many actual inscriptions, but rarely is anything simple in the poetry of Callimachus.

III (GP 49, AP 7.458, Pf 50)

An epitaph for a nursemaid. Mikkos means "little one" and was probably a baby name; the real name of the man is not given. Aischre means "ugly." The poem has many of the features of an inscription, but its seriousness is belied at the beginning of the poem by the reference to Aischre as "Good-Milk," an affectionate if somewhat direct name for a wet nurse. The last line leaves little doubt that the poem was intended to be humorous. Theocritus also wrote an epitaph for a nursemaid whose tombstone was set up by a Mikkos (epigram III), and we have a third poem for a nursemaid from the Hellenistic poet Dioscorides (see also Posidippus II). It is possible that all of these poems belonged to a series of variants by Hellenistic poets on this theme, most of which have now been lost.

IV and V (GP 29, AP 7.525, Pf 21 and GP 30, AP 7.415, Pf 35)

These two epigrams make a clever pair. The first is for the father of Callimachus the poet, who is the son of a man also named Callimachus, a general in the army of Cyrene. This first poem is in the form of an epitaph, but it says almost nothing about the person actually buried and doesn't even give his name (see also Theocritus I). The second poem is for Battiades: that is, "son of Battos." The poet Callimachus was known by this patronymic among Latin poets—for example, he was named as Battiades in Catullus 65 and 116. According to the *Suda,* Callimachus was called Battiades because Battos was his father's name. Many commentators therefore believe that this second poem supplies the name of the deceased missing from the first epitaph. But the *Suda* cannot always be trusted. Because Battos was also the name of the legendary founder of Cyrene, "Battiades" may simply mean "from Cyrene." In whatever way we interpret the patronymic, the second poem is a "self-epitaph"; it says that Callimachus could combine wine and laughter in due measure, taking the middle path between the distrust of drunkenness in Posidippus XII and the carousing in Asclepiades XX. In line 3, "to sing" means "to write verse," as often in Greek and Latin poetry.

VI (GP 31, AP 7.524, Pf 13)

This epigram gives the name of the buried man and his patronymic just as an actual epitaph would do, but the poem is in every other respect far removed from the inscriptional tradition. Many inscriptions begin with the tombstone addressing the passerby, but here the passerby addresses the tombstone and then, after confirming that Charidas is buried within, turns to converse with him instead of with the grave marker. Unlike an actual epitaph, the poem says nothing about Charidas himself but is a humorous disquisition on the likelihood of life after death. The low cost of living in the underworld was proverbial among the Greeks. The Greek word used in the poem for "penny" is *Pellaios,* a coin of low denomination from Pella, the capital of Macedonia. Although there is considerable controversy about what these last two lines mean, there is some evidence that such a coin may have been stamped with the figure of an ox. So Callimachus may be saying that in the underworld, an "ox" can be traded for an ox.

VII and VIII (GP 51, AP 7.317, Pf 4 and GP 52, AP 7.318, Pf 3)

Timon was a familiar figure in Greek literature and a favorite subject for epitaphs: eight are preserved in the *Greek Anthology,* including these two of Callimachus. Timon is the subject of Shakespeare's play *Timon of Athens,* which was based in part on the dialogue *Timon* by Lucian, a second-century CE Greek essayist. Part of the story is also told in Plutarch's *Life of Antony.* Timon was probably an historical figure, an Athenian who lived in the time of Aristophanes and the Peloponnesian War. He was a wealthy man who was ruined by too much generosity to men he thought were his friends, and as a consequence he forever after conceived a hatred for all men. Plutarch says that the inscription on Timon's tombstone actually read

> Pressed by a heavy blow,
> My life thread severed, here I lie;
> My name you shall not know.
> In ruin may you scoundrels die!

These two mock epitaphs by Callimachus also incorporate Timon's reputation for misanthropy. The first begins with the poet or passerby addressing the deceased, who then responds (as in VI). The frank admission "since you are no longer" acknowledges Timon's insubstantiality and draws attention to and pokes fun at the convention of the talking gravestone. Timon says in the poem that he prefers being alive because he doesn't like other people, and "There's more of you in Hell." This logic reflects the assumption that the number of the dead greatly exceeds that of the living (see also Leonidas XII and note). The second poem seems almost to be a continuation of the first; it depends upon it, since the name of the deceased is not given. These two poems appeared close to one another in the *Greek Anthology,* and they may have been nearby or even adjacent in Meleager's *Garland* and in Callimachus's own book of poetry.

IX (GP 32, AP 7.517, Pf 20)

The next four epigrams I have translated make no pretense of being actual epitaphs. This first poem on the children of Aristippos may describe people Callimachus actually knew. Cyrene was of course Callimachus's hometown, and the names Aristippos and Melanippos both appear on its coins from the late fourth and early third century. The family of Aristippos may therefore have been upper-class (like Callimachus) and of some political importance. This inference is supported by the poem: the city of Cyrene would hardly have mourned with Aristippos if he had been a shopkeeper or a minor official.

X (GP 44, AP 7.519, Pf 14)

Charmis is a young man who has died suddenly and *aoros,* "before his time." The epigram has many similarities to the preceding poem. The voice is again that of an observer of the burial, reflecting on the sadness of loss, and the focus of the poem is similarly on the grief of the father, who must bear the pain of his child's untimely death.

XI (GP 40, AP 7.522, Pf 15)

In this poem we are perhaps meant to imagine a statue above the tomb with the name Timonoe below it. The poet, reading the epitaph, only gradually realizes who this Timonoe is and expresses his own sadness at her parting. This epigram reflects the great affection of many Greek husbands for their wives, which is amply attested in actual surviving epitaphs on tombstones. Greek men did not treat their wives as equals, often not consulting them in important decisions, but ties of genuine love could be just as strong then as now.

XII (GP 34, AP 7.80, Pf 2)

Almost nothing is known about Heraclitus of Halicarnassus, the subject of this affecting poem. Diogenes Laertius calls him a poet of "elegy"— that is, of poems in elegiac meter, which included epigrams. *Nightingales* was presumably the title of a collection of his poems, all of which have sadly disappeared except for a single epigram preserved in Meleager's *Garland* (*AP* 7.465).

XIII (GP 17, AP 13.7, Pf 37)

The next seven poems I have selected are closely related to the tradition of dedication epigrams. I begin, as I did for epitaphs, with a poem most like an actual inscription. Cretans were famous in antiquity as archers;

one such archer, who was perhaps a mercenary, dedicates his quiver and bow made of horn to the god Serapis, but he does not include his arrows, since they are all in the bodies of his foe. Serapis, originally a god of the underworld looking in some statues much like Hades with the three-headed dog Cerberus at his feet, with time acquired more of the attributes of Zeus. He is usually shown with a basket of grain on his head, symbolizing fertility. The Hesperitai were the people who lived in Hesperis (or Hesperides), a city on the coast of Africa now called Benghazi and the second-largest city in modern Libya.

XIV (GP 23, AP 6.146, Pf 53)

Eileithyia was the daughter of Zeus and Hera and the Greek goddess of childbirth. Women dedicated gifts to her in the hope of alleviating labor pains or in thankfulness after a successful delivery. In an actual inscription probably written about a hundred years before this poem, a woman dedicates a statue to Eileithyia and asks for her goodwill in return, much as does Lykainis. What makes Callimachus's poem different is the ever so diplomatic suggestion, that although Lykainis appreciates the help of the goddess in her just-completed labor and is thankful for her baby girl, she would be even more grateful if next time around the goddess could manage to bring a boy. No woman would actually risk inscribing such a sentiment on a gift in a temple, since it would seem unappreciative, and this unexpected twist provides the humor of the poem.

XV (GP 28, AP 6.301, Pf 47)

A salt tub is a storage container generally made of wood, in which salt could be placed and pounded. A diet of salt and bread was a frugal diet (see, for example, Leonidas XXVIII), and by means of his economy Eudemos escaped from his debt. Samothrace is an island in the northern Aegean Sea, and the gods of Samothrace were the Cabeiri, originally Phrygian gods of fertility and protectors of sailors from shipwreck and bad weather, who were worshipped in the Ptolemaic court. The poem plays on the tradition of dedication epigrams by seamen made in thankfulness after return from a successful voyage. Eudemos escaped "storms of debt" and commends his salt tub to the Cabeiri, saying he was "saved from the sea." This is something a sailor might say, but here Eudemos means that he was saved *by means of* the sea—that is, by the salt he used in his thrifty diet. This sense is clearer in Greek, because the word Callimachus uses, *hals,* can mean both "sea" and "salt," a pun impossible to render in English.

XVI (GP 26, AP 6.310, Pf 48)

This poem is similar to Asclepiades III and was probably modeled upon it. A theatrical mask is again hung by a boy in a schoolroom as a dedication to the Muses, but in the poem of Asclepiades the mask is comic and here it is tragic. Simos, which means "snub-nosed," was a surprisingly common name. Glaukos was a captain in the Lycian army, who fought in support of the Trojans before Troy. In a famous scene in book 6 of the *Iliad,* Glaukos meets the Greek warrior Diomedes, who, upon discovering that Glaukos is the grandson of Bellerophon, puts down his sword and declares his friendship. Homer says that Zeus took away the wits of Glaukos, so that he exchanged his gold armor worth one hundred oxen for Diomedes' bronze armor worth only nine. This encounter later became proverbial. The poem thus is saying that the Muses, like Glaukos, gave away something of value (Simon's good marks) for something worth far less (the mask). The mouth of the mask—open, as are all theatrical masks—here gapes in boredom, though it is unclear why the mask would gape twice as wide as might the Samian god. It is usually supposed that this is a reference to a tale then current, which has come down to us from a later account in Pliny the Elder's *Natural History.* A Samian man named Elpis is said to have come to Africa by ship, and after encountering a lion near the shore he climbed a tree in fright and prayed to Bacchus. He then noticed that the lion had a bone stuck in his throat, so he descended and was able to remove it. The lion in turn provided Elpis's ship with game, and Elpis later dedicated a temple to Bacchus on Samos. If this is the intended allusion, one cannot help but wonder why in the poem the mouth of Samian Bacchus gaped open and not that of the lion. Perhaps a statue of Bacchus in the temple on Samos represented the god in this fashion. The phrase "my locks are sacred" comes from Euripides' play *The Bacchae* (line 494), where it is spoken by Bacchus. The mask during its years of service must have heard this line countless times.

XVII (GP 25, AP 6.149, Pf 56)

As in many actual inscriptions (and the preceding epigram), the object that has been dedicated speaks to the reader and describes the circumstances of the dedication. The statue in the poem says that Euainetos has dedicated it, a bronze cock, in return for victory, presumably in a cockfighting contest. Public cockfighting contests were held in the theater in Athens and probably in many other locations in Greece as well. The cock also says, however, that it can't really be sure of any of this but is taking the word of Euainetos. The poem questions our assumptions about the role of a speaking object in a dedication inscription (see chapter 1).

XVIII (GP 22, AP 6.351, Pf 34)

In this poem Callimachus plays even more outrageously with the traditions of dedication inscriptions. The epigram again begins with the object of the dedication speaking, this time a club of oak dedicated to Hercules. After making its initial announcement, however, the club is suddenly and peremptorily interrupted by Hercules and is asked who is making the dedication and which Archinos this is. Once Hercules has been satisfied by the club's responses, he accepts the dedication. The novelty and wit of the poem come from its use of dialogue, and from the unconventional way Callimachus employs this untraditional format to provide the name and country of the person making the dedication, essential information in any actual inscription. The lion is the Nemean lion, whose killing was the first of the twelve labors of Hercules. The skin of this beast was so tough that no weapon could penetrate it, and Hercules was compelled to wrestle it and choke it to death. He is often portrayed with the skin of the lion draped over his shoulder and with a club. The swine is the Erymanthian boar, which in another of Hercules' labors was captured alive and then slain.

XIX (GP 24, AP 6.147, Pf 54)

This last of the dedication epigrams I have included isn't really a dedication epigram at all. Asclepius is the Greek god of medicine, and Akeson has been visiting one of the god's shrines (see notes to Posidippus XXVII–XXX). Although there was no entry fee to the temples of Asclepius, gifts to the shrine were expected—particularly in the case of a cure. The epigram of Akeson is inscribed on a tablet, and we know that such tablets were customarily placed along the pathways of the temples by grateful patients. This particular tablet, however, does not describe a patient's recovery or the dedication of a gift in appreciation but is rather an attestation of payment. The source of humor is the transformation of a god into a simple businessman, with the evident implication that the god (and his minions) cannot be trusted to remember when they have been paid and might perhaps be just a tad greedy.

XX (GP 1, AP 12.102, Pf 31)

The next nine poems are all on erotic subjects and include some of the most famous poems of Callimachus. In this first love epigram, we are perhaps meant to imagine the poet at a symposium where sex is freely available, explaining to his drinking companion Epikydes why he doesn't take what is on offer. This epigram was well known to ancient readers and translated in part by Horace (in *Satires* 1.2.105–8), who however rejects Callimachus's conclusion and argues instead in favor of cheap prostitutes (see also Philodemos V). When I first translated the poem, I made the ending like this:

> If someone says, "Look, there's a wounded doe,"
> He does not take it. Love's like that for me:
> I only chase the one who tries to flee.

This gives the poem more "point" and a structure closer to our modern conception of an epigram, but such a pithy ending would be quite unfaithful to the Greek. In this poem and in many of his other epigrams, Callimachus did not seek the sort of concision common for example in the epigrams of Martial and Ben Jonson. Perhaps he felt that if all of his poems ended with point, they would collectively become tedious to the reader, an effect he may have attempted to avoid by varying the structure from one epigram to the next.

XXI (GP 2, AP 12.43, Pf 28)

This poem begins with a theme similar to the one before: the poet professes his dislike for anything that is ordinary, whether in poetry or in love. In the prologue to his long elegiac poem the *Aitia* (or *Causes*), Callimachus describes himself taking a writing tablet on his lap for the first time, and recounts how Apollo (the god of poetry) told him not to lead his chariot along the same tracks others have followed but to take roads that have not been worn down, even if these are narrower. Apollo's advice was to take the road "less traveled by," and the poetry of Callimachus is distinguished by its novelty and originality. In this epigram the poet is expressing a similar view, which he then extends from literature to his love life. The cyclic poems were epic poems written to fill in the events of the story of the Trojan War that occurred before, between, and after the *Iliad* and *Odyssey*. Only fragments of these poems have survived, but they were generally held by the ancients to be inferior to Homer's. The irony of the epigram comes from the definitive rejection at the beginning of the poem of whatever is ordinary, followed by an erotic compliment directed at the boy Lysanies. We expect Callimachus to end the poem by saying that Lysanies may look great, but that the boy has clearly been around the block and is just the sort of lover Callimachus rejects. Or perhaps that Lysanies looks great but not in any ordinary way. What the poet says, of course, is that Lysanies looks great, but that someone else got there first. So much for good intentions! In Greek, the name Lysanies means "reliever of pain or sorrow" and was certainly intended to be ironic. Many scholars believe that the phrase "someone's got him" in the last line, *allos echei,* is intended to be a muffled echo of "beautiful, yes" (*kalos naichi*) from the line above. I have made no attempt to imitate that effect in English.

XXII (GP 4, AP 12.73, Pf 41)

The beginning of this epigram is based on Asclepiades VII, though the desperation in that poem has been replaced here by playful sophistication. Aristotle in the first book of his *Nicomachean Ethics* describes the soul as divided into rational and irrational parts, often at odds with one another. The notion that one part of the soul could go looking for the other, as one looks for a runaway slave, gives an amusing conceit to this familiar theme. Callimachus the poet writes with superb control of his technique about Callimachus the lover, who is so out of control that he has quite literally lost his mind (or at least half of it). This poem was apparently well-known to the Romans since it was translated by Quintus Lutatius Catulus, a general and consul unrelated to the poet Catullus and probably writing near 100 BCE, when many believe that Meleager's *Garland* arrived in Rome. The reading of Callimachus's epigram is uncertain, and the one I have adopted is based in part on the text of Catulus's ancient translation. The poem appears to be saying that we should look for the missing half of the poet's soul at the house of Theutimos, presumably intended to be the name of an adolescent with whom the poet has lately fallen in love.

XXIII (GP 6, AP 12.230, Pf 52)

This poem may also have been partly based on a poem by Asclepiades and is one of the most charming of the love epigrams of Callimachus. The poet pleads with Zeus to show favor to Theocritus if Theocritus returns the poet's love. Zeus was notorious in antiquity for his love affairs (see, for example, Asclepiades XII), and one of his most famous liaisons was with the boy Ganymede, a Trojan prince who was brought by Zeus to Olympus and became his lover and cupbearer. The poet mentions this affair in support of his own suffering but tactfully abstains from elaboration.

XXIV (GP 7, AP 12.148, Pf 32)

Attractive young boys were often criticized in antiquity for selling themselves to the highest bidder, and Menippos seems to be among their number. What makes this poem touching is the poet's frank admission that he cannot satisfy his lover's expectations, and his hurt and disappointment when Menippos insists on pointing out the obvious.

XXV (GP 8, AP 12.118, Pf 42)

This poem was discovered in mutilated form as an inscription (probably from the first century CE) on the wall of a house on the Esquiline Hill, an expensive residential district rising above the Colosseum in Rome. It resembles Asclepiades XIII in mood and shows Callimachus at his very best. As in Posidippus VIII, the poet arrives inebriated at the door of his beloved but is apologetic rather than vainglorious and does not ask to be let in. The apology seems to presage some horrible deed, such as breaking down the door or setting fire to the house. We then learn that "the poet has merely indulged in a harmless sentimental gesture," as Giangrande put it. The complexity of feeling rivals the best of the love poetry of the Latin poet Catullus.

XXVI (GP 9, AP 12.139, Pf 44)

The ashes and fire of love are familiar from Posidippus IX and Asclepia-des VI, VII, XVII, and XX. What gives the poem its poignancy is the poet's admission that he is powerless to alter his feeling. The "fire beneath these ashes" suggests a prior love affair from which he seems never to have recovered. Instead of steeling his own resolve, as Posidip-pus attempts to do in epigrams X–XII, Callimachus acknowledges his helplessness and places the responsibility entirely upon the shoulders of his lover. The reader can only wish him the best of luck. The reading of the poem is uncertain, and some scholars propose that Menexenos is an observer or friend rather than Callimachus's purported lover. But since the names given in so many of the other love poems belong to boys with whom Callimachus claims to be infatuated, I have assumed that to be the case in this poem as well; and following a suggestion of Gow and Page I have read the verb of the last sentence as being in the second person, *buleis,* rather than the third person, *balei* or *ballei* (as in the *Palatine Anthology*).

XXVII and XXVIII (GP 12, AP 12.71, Pf 30 and GP 13, AP 12.134, Pf 43)

These two poem have a similar theme. The poet in the first expresses surprise and shock that Kleonikos is reduced to skin and hair, and he then infers from his own experience that these are symptoms of over-whelming passion. The poet in the second poem (based on Asclepiades XIV) sees the sighing and heavy drinking of a guest at a dinner party and concludes that that man, too, is in love, though trying to keep it secret. Both these poems of Callimachus are written in a style similar to the one used by Asclepiades, with short sentences, sudden interrogatives, and a sharply focused ending.

XXIX *(GP 59, AP 11.362, Pf 59)*

The poet compares himself to Orestes, who was the son of Agamemnon and Clytemnestra and whose life was the subject of some of the greatest plays of Athenian tragedy. During Agamemnon's ten-year absence from Mycenae during the Trojan War, Clytemnestra had an affair with Aegisthus and sent Orestes to Phocis to be raised in the household of King Strophius. There Orestes became the fast friend of Strophius's son Pylades, a friendship that became proverbial. This is presumably why in the poem Orestes is said to have been "lucky." After Clytemnestra murdered Agamemnon, Pylades returned to Mycenae with Orestes and helped him kill Clytemnestra and Aegisthus. Orestes was then pursued by the Furies and driven mad—as the poem says, "crazy . . . though not like me." Callimachus seems to imply that he himself was crazy because he wrote a play. The *Suda* says that Callimachus wrote comedies and tragedies, though there are no examples among his surviving works. The point of the poem seems to be that Orestes never really tested his friendship with Pylades, since he never tried his hand at drama. It is unclear why his friendship would have been tested—perhaps from his friend's jealousy if the play had been successful, or from his friend's false praise or too frank truthfulness if it had not.

XXX *(GP 54, AP 7.89, Pf 1)*

Pittakos was born in the middle of the seventh century BCE in Mytilene on the island of Lesbos, and he was an army commander and ruler who became widely known as one of the seven sages of ancient Greece. In *Lives of the Philosophers* Diogenes Laertius cites Callimachus's epigram and says that Pittakos may have given the advice of the poem from his own experience of marriage, since he married above his station and his wife never let him forget it. The boys in Callimachus's poem tell the tops to "keep to your own way" so they will avoid striking one another, since collisions often cause the tops to precess and tumble to the ground. Dion was a common name.

CHAPTER SEVEN

Theocritus

Theocritus was born about 300 BCE in the important Greek city of Syracuse in Sicily, but he spent much of his life further east in Alexandria. One of his poems describes the streets and palace of the Egyptian capital in some detail, and another is addressed to Ptolemy. Theocritus may also have spent some time on the island of Kos near Rhodes, where he seems to have met the doctor Nikias, who appears in several of his poems (see epigram VIII). Theocritus is most famous for his "bucolic" or pastoral poetry, which was included in a collection of longer poems called *Idylls*. He may not have been the first pastoral poet, but his poems about shepherds and cowherds provided the stimulus for Virgil's *Eclogues* and the whole of the pastoral tradition in European literature. The pastoral poems, however, represent only part of the *Idylls*. Some of the other poems in that collection are dramatic mimes, presenting a sharply drawn comic scene. Others are narrative, including two about Hercules. There are in addition a hymn to the gods Castor and Pollux and several poems of an occasional nature, including love poems to boys.

Theocritus also wrote epigrams. These poems were not a part of Meleager's *Garland* but have come down to us in ancient manuscripts of Theocritus's bucolic poetry and in the *Greek Anthology*, where they appear in several distinct groups. That Meleager did not include the epigrams of Theocritus in the *Garland* (but did select a few poems by Theocritus's friend Nikias) has caused some scholars to doubt whether Theocritus actually wrote the epigrams attributed to him, and a few of the poems may be spurious. The majority, however, including those I have translated, are very likely to be genuine. They are for the most part typical productions of a Hellenistic poet and show clear affinities with poems of other third-century authors, particularly Anyte, Leonidas, and Callimachus. The epigrams that have survived are mostly epitaphs and dedications, though there are also epideictic epigrams, including poems of a rural character.

Our evidence would suggest that Theocritus was a member of a circle in Alexandria that included many of the most important literary figures of his day. According to one source Theocritus was a pupil of Asclepiades, and in one of Theocritus's pastoral poems (*Idyll* 7) a character perhaps intended to represent Theocritus himself says that he is no match for Asclepiades, the great poet of the island of Samos. Theocritus never mentions Callimachus by name, but a comparison of their epigrams reveals many similarities. Both wrote epitaphs for nursemaids (Theocritus III, Callimachus III) whose tombs were purportedly erected by someone with the same nickname—Mikkos, or "little one." Callimachus wrote an epigram (IX) about an adolescent girl who killed herself in grief after her brother died; Theocritus wrote a similar poem (epigram II), but about a girl only six years old. In both poems, the focus is on the grief of a parent, the father in Callimachus but the mother in Theocritus. Theocritus wrote an epigram (I) for a son that says nothing about him, does not even give his name, and praises only the son's father. Callimachus wrote a similar epigram but this time for a father (IV), his own father, which again does not give the name of the deceased and says nothing about him.

Theocritus resembles Callimachus in other ways as well. Both used traditional meters and forms for a new kind of poetry, and there is a subtlety in the work of both poets that is often easy to miss. When we read Theocritus's *Idylls,* we must constantly be on the alert for context and hidden meaning. That is equally true of his epigrams. One of my favorites is IV, an epitaph for a man called Orthon. The English scholar A. S. F. Gow, who edited all of Theocritus's poems, says of epigram IV that it is "probably a genuine epitaph." Our first suspicion to the contrary is the name itself, *Orthon,* which in Greek means "erect" or "upright," from which our word "orthogonal" comes. But "upright" is one thing Orthon isn't! The poem purports to warn the reader not to go about drunk on a stormy winter night, for if he does, he will end up as Orthon says he has, buried in some foreign place rather than in his own "great fatherland." This seems to be a simple message of prudent advice until we realize that Orthon is from Syracuse, the city where Theocritus himself was born. We may then begin to wonder whether Theocritus is intimating that his countrymen are, like Orthon, mostly drunks and braggarts. Or whether Theocritus wrote the Orthon epitaph to make fun of his foreign friends, lamenting poor Orthon, who could have been buried in a "great fatherland" like Syracuse instead of some dump like Alexandria or Kos. It is impossible for us now to know what the poet had in mind, but what we *can* say is that this poem, like the "epitaphs" of Leonidas and Callimachus, was very likely *not* a genuine inscription. All of these epigrams share a clever and often charming richness and sophistication that is characteristic of Hellenistic poetry.

I

You left an infant son, and now he too,
A young man, Eurymédon, is with you,
Dead in this tomb. Your place is with the blessed,
    But townsfolk will to him convey
    Their honor and esteem, when they
Recall the worth his father had possessed.

II

Life for this girl of six too soon was done,
She went to Hades with life scarce begun,
Missing, poor girl, her baby brother, who
Had tasted heartless death, though not yet two.
Alas, Peristeré! How near the blow
That fate can give to men of darkest woe!

III

When Médeios, called "Míkkos," this tomb made
For his Thracian nurse beside the road, he bade
Them carve "of Kleíta" on the marker stone.
Solicitude the woman once had shown
When he was young, this grave will now repay.
And why not? Of her, "helpful" they'll still say.

IV

Oh stranger, this from Orthon, who
   Once came from Syracuse to you,
     And now gives his advice:

   Don't go out on a winter night,
When you're more than a little tight,
     And the weather isn't nice;

Or in some foreign place you'll lie,
Not your great fatherland, as I
Who pay this fateful price.

V

Hippónax the poet lies here.
If wicked, then do not come near.
If honest, a good name you keep,
Sit down. If you wish, go to sleep.

VI

The chorus leader Damoménes, who
Gave this tripod and statuette of you,
Oh Dionysus, sweetest of the blessed,
Was moderate in everything, possessed
For men the choral victory, and could
See what was suitable and what was good.

VII

This pleasing gift to all you nine,
This marble statue, goddesses, for your shrine
Does Xenoklés bestow.
He is your protégé,
No one will say
It isn't so.
Praised for his skill and art,
He keeps the Muses ever close to his heart.

VIII

Apollo's son to Míletos once came
To meet Nikías, hearing of his fame
As healer of the sick, and that he prayed
Each day with sacrifices, and had made
This statue, pledging the top price to pay
For Eëtíon's fine hand, to defray
The cost of carving fragrant cedarwood.
The sculptor gave it all the craft he could.

IX

To citizens and foreigners, the same
Consideration gives this bank. Reclaim
Whatever sum the abacus produces!
Another banker, let him make excuses!
But when they want it, Kaikos pays what's right
With someone else's cash, even at night.

X

You slumber, Daphnis, on a leaf-strewn bed;
    Your tired body now is still,
    Your hunting stakes fixed on the hill.
But Pan and Priapus, on whose lovely head

Sits crocus-colored ivy as a crown,
    Come to this cave to look for you,
    With like intent. So flee! Subdue
The drowsy deepening that pulls you down.

XI

The Muses have the roses wet with dew,
And this thick creeping thyme; and then for you,
Apollo, there are dark-leaved boughs of bay,
Since Delphic rock has that as your display.
This horned white goat will make an altar red,
Who with the tips of terebinth is fed.

XII

Look closely at this statue, stranger; say,
Once you've from Teos homeward made your way,
    "I saw Anacreon, the best
        of all the poets past."
You will complete the man by adding,
        "and a pederast."

EXPLANATORY NOTES

I (GP 8, AP 7.659, BG 7)

This is an epitaph for the grave of a father and his son, and it superficially resembles many actual inscriptions for tombs that contain several members of one family. That the son died in his prime is a common theme. What makes the poem quite unlike an actual inscription, however, is the scant attention given to the son, whose name isn't even mentioned. An actual epitaph is an occasion for praise of the deceased, but the only good thing the poet has to say about the son is that he had a worthy father. This poem may have been the model for an epitaph of Callimachus (epigram IV). The focus of that poem is similarly not on the deceased but rather on Callimachus himself and his father's father, whose accomplishments are much lauded. But of the father himself nothing is said. There is some dispute about the text of this poem; I have adopted the reading of Gallavotti and Rossi.

II (GP 9, AP 7.662, BG 16)

This affecting poem for a girl and her baby brother is similar to epigram IX of Callimachus—so similar that Callimachus's poem may have served as its model. Callimachus writes about a girl in Cyrene who took her life after her brother died, and his poem may have been based on a family he actually knew. In the epigram of Theocritus we have a similar occasion, but here the siblings are unexpectedly young. We can perhaps barely imagine a child of six dying of grief for her baby brother, but the circumstances seem rather unusual; it is more likely that Theocritus's poem was not intended to be taken at face value but rather was meant as a humorous variation on the poem of Callimachus, turning the subject of that earlier epigram into a *reductio ad absurdum*. This may seem to us now in rather poor taste, but modern preferences can often be a misleading guide to the practices of Hellenistic poets. The "poor Peristere" has been supposed by some to be the six-year-old girl; though that reading is possible, there is strong reason to believe that she is instead the mother mourning the loss of her children. The last couplet of Callimachus IX describes the grief of the father of the dead children, and in keeping with the Hellenistic practice of *variatio* Theocritus is probably doing the same here but for the mother. It is unlikely to be mere coincidence that the names of the parents appear in the same line in both epigrams, in Greek and in my translations. Peristere means "pigeon" or "dove."

III (GP 11, AP 7.663, BG 20)

Another epigram closely related to a poem of Callimachus (epigram III). The nickname Mikkos means "small" or "little" in Doric and is used elsewhere in Theocritus of an infant child. As a baby Medeios may have been called Mikkos by his nurse, perhaps as a term of endearment. Thracian slaves often served as wet nurses; the name of the nurse, Kleita, means "famous" or "illustrious." This poem seems at first glance to be an epitaph for the nurse, but on closer reading we see that only the words "of

Kleita" or perhaps "of helpful Kleita" are said to be carved on the grave marker, and not the remainder of the epigram. Short inscriptions consisting of names in the genitive were sometimes placed on tombstones belonging to a slave or woman of low status such as a wet nurse, when indeed anything was engraved at all.

IV (GP 12, AP 7.660, BG 9)

This poem is discussed in the introduction to this chapter. For the choice of the name Orthon ("Erect" or "Upright") for a man lying in a grave, see Posidippus XXIV, where Euelthon (Well-traveling) ignores an unfavorable omen and dies on a journey; Callimachus XXI, where Lysanies (Relieving Distress) instead provokes it; and Lucillius XXIX, where Makron (Tall) is so short that a mouse drags him to a mouse hole.

V (GP 13, AP 13.3, BG 19)

Another in the series of Hellenistic epigrams intended as fictitious epitaphs of famous poets. We have already encountered a similar poem by Leonidas (epigram XIII) on the Greek iambic poet Hipponax, whose verses were famous for biting satire of his contemporaries.

VI (GP 4, AP 6.339, BG 12)

This poem combines aspects of several different types of epigram. It celebrates a victory in choral song and is also a dedication epigram to Dionysus, but near the end it reads almost like an epitaph. Damomenes was a *choregos,* or "chorus leader"—the person who defrayed the costs of producing a choral performance. He won a competition for the men's chorus, whose prize was a bronze tripod (a three-legged cauldron). Within the tripod stood a figure of Dionysus (Bacchus), suggesting that the victory was obtained at a festival in honor of that god. At the Dionysia in Athens, choruses of boys and men drawn each from one of the Athenian tribes competed, and the victorious tribe won a tripod. The songs they sang, called dithyrambs, were primarily (perhaps exclusively) in praise of the god Dionysus and became the forerunners of Greek tragedy. The second half of the epigram praises Damomenes for his moderation and good sense, and this part of the poem by itself could easily have appeared on a tombstone. Theocritus may be trying to show that an epigram need not be only a victory inscription or a dedication or an epitaph but can be all three together.

VII (GP 3, AP 6.338, BG 10)

Another dedication, from a man called Xenokles the *mousikos*. The word *mousikos* can mean "musician" but can also apply more generally to any protégé of the Muses, such as a poet or a man of letters or even a scholar. Xenokles seems somewhat defensive, careful to say that no one would dispute his claim to be a *mousikos* and eager to let us know that he has been praised for his skill. Vainglory is not at all rare in actual dedication epigrams, particularly for those who have won athletic victories (see introduction to chapter 10); many actual inscriptions of this kind survive. It is amusing to picture Theocritus writing this poem for some particularly obnoxious minor poet, but the circumstances of the epigram are completely unknown.

VIII (GP 1, AP 6.337, BG 8)

The son of Apollo referred to in the beginning of the poem is Asclepius, who in mythology was the god of medicine and worshipped in many parts of Greece, probably first at his sanctuary at Epidaurus (see note to Posidippus XXVII). Miletos was an important Greek town in Ionia south of Ephesus, on what is now the coast of Turkey. Nikias was a doctor and a friend of Theocritus, mentioned in several other of his poems. He was apparently born in Miletos but may have met Theocritus on the nearby island of Kos, the birthplace of Hippocrates, when Nikias was attending the medical school there. Theocritus's claim in this epigram that Asclepius traveled to Miletos to be with Nikias was presumably a testament to Nikias's high reputation and devotion. But though it initially seems to take the form of a dedication, the poem becomes ecphrastic and gives a description of the statue that is being dedicated. There is a curious emphasis on the cost of the statue, as in Callimachus *Iambi* 6 (see introduction to chapter 6). Theocritus may have been giving his rich friend a hard time about his extravagance. Successful doctors in ancient Greece are known to have been paid quite well.

IX (GP 18, AP 9.435, BG 14)

This epideictic epigram, like Posidippus XXVI, is a rare example of a purported sign or advertisement. The sign reassures potential clients that visitors from foreign cities are treated just as well as actual citizens. This promise was important, since itinerant merchants in Hellenistic Greece often deposited sums in banks to have cash readily available in the various cities where they traded goods. If the merchant's own deposit happened not to be easily accessible, Kaikos pledges to use the money of other clients to pay off the claim. Kaikos's emphasis on accuracy and ease of withdrawal suggests that honesty among Greek bankers may not have been universal. Being open at night could have been especially important in a seaport like Alexandria, because prevailing winds might have kept sailors from coming into port before nightfall.

X (GP 19, AP 9.338, BG 3)

This poem may have been written as an inscription for a painting or statue group, but it could also be an occasional poem of description and narration with a rural theme. Daphnis appears elsewhere in Theocritus and in Greek literature as the child of a nymph and as the fabled inventor of pastoral song, who became a herdsman and not (as in this epigram) a hunter. The "like intent" of Pan and Priapus is certainly amorous. In his commentary on this poem (in *Theocritus*), Gow mentions an ancient Greek vase by the Pan Painter showing a goatherd chased by Pan, while a small statue or herm of Priapus looks on. The theme of this epigram may thus have been relatively common.

XI (GP 5, AP 6.336, BG 1)

Another poem perhaps written as an inscription to a painting or statue group. The laurel leaves of the bay tree were sacred to Apollo and were used to crown the victors at the Pythian games at Delphi, given in Apollo's honor. Terebinth is a small tree from which turpentine is tapped and whose young leaves are edible (at least to goats).

XII (GP 15, AP 9.599, BG 17)

The lyric poet Anacreon was a favorite subject of Greek epigram; among poets mentioned in the poems of the *Greek Anthology* only Homer appears more frequently. We have already encountered an epigram on Anacreon by Leonidas (XXIV). That poem is ecphrastic in the narrowest sense of the word, giving a detailed description of a work of art almost as if the poet were standing before it. The present epigram of Theocritus is clearly modeled on that poem: it is also about a statue of Anacreon, perhaps the same one described by Leonidas, which Theocritus says is in Teos, Anacreon's hometown north of Ephesus on the coast of present-day Turkey. The epigram of Theocritus begins almost like an epitaph with an address to the passerby, who is asked to take a message home (much as in Asclepiades II). What the passerby is asked to convey, however, is not information about a burial but rather a description of a work of art. But if the passerby does this faithfully, his description of the poet will not be complete unless he also mentions Anacreon's fondness for boys. Since Theocritus himself wrote love poems to boys, he probably would have approved of Anacreon's proclivity. The Greek word *paiderastes* means literally "lover of boys" and did not always have the negative connotation now attached to "pederast."

CHAPTER EIGHT

Meleager

Meleager tells us (in epigram I) that he was born in Coele-Syria or Pales-
tine in a city called Gadara, now Umm Qais in present-day Lebanon.
Gadara was one of ten cities collectively known as the Decapolis, founded
by Greek settlers in land conquered by Alexander the Great and occu-
pied mostly by people of Semitic descent (including Jews), in much the
way Alexandria was established in Egypt. Earlier critics such as Henri
Ouvré explained some of the characteristics of Meleager's verse from his
birth and upbringing in the Middle East, calling them "Syrian," but this
is somewhat like calling the poetry of Callimachus "Libyan." Although

there is some evidence that the religion and practices of local cultures were assimilated by the Hellenistic Greeks in the Middle East, for the most part the Greek rulers and colonizers brought their customs with them and had as little to do with the "natives" as possible. Cleopatra, though often depicted in the popular imagination as a dark-skinned Egyptian, was in fact a Macedonian Greek. She spoke Egyptian, but according to Plutarch she was the first of the Ptolemies in more than two hundred years to have bothered to learn the language. That Meleager says "hail" or "greetings" at the end of one of his poems in three different languages, including Syrian, is sometimes adduced as evidence that he could speak the local dialect. This is of course possible, though my knowing how to say *adiós amigos* doesn't mean I can speak Spanish. Meleager was an intelligent and well-educated member of the Greek diaspora who inherited all of the traditions of Greek poetry from Homer onward. His verse displays no clear evidence of Syrian influence.

At some point in his youth, Meleager's family must have left Gadara, since he says that it was the Phoenician coastal town of Tyre that "nursed him" and "reared him to manhood." Most of his love poems to boys were written in Tyre (see notes to IV–XIV), and this may be true of much of his love poetry to women as well. Meleager tells us that when he reached old age, he was made a citizen of the Greek island of Kos. Since Kos is mentioned in epigrams Meleager included in the *Garland,* he must have written these poems (as well as the introductory and concluding poems of the *Garland*) and assembled his anthology on Kos during his declining years. His dates are uncertain, but most scholars now believe that the *Garland* was written and appeared in Rome at the beginning of the first century BCE. Meleager was therefore probably born about 160–150 BCE and died after 90 BCE; he lived more than a century later than all the other poets we have so far considered.

Meleager says (in epigram I) that his first literary effort was the composition of a book called the *Charites* or *Graces,* which he calls "Menippean" in honor of the Cynic philosopher Menippus. Like Meleager, Menippus lived in Gadara but much earlier, in the first half of the third century BCE;

he wrote satires in a combination of poetry and prose in a style called *spou-daiogeloion,* or "serious comedy" (see the introduction to chapter 3 and notes to Leonidas VI and XVIII). The *Graces* of Meleager were probably also written in this style, though only a few fragments have survived. In one passage, Meleager is said to have explained that the heroes of the *Iliad* did not eat fish even though it was abundant in the waters off Troy, because Homer was a Syrian and Syrians don't eat fish. This was clearly meant as a joke. No one knows where Homer came from, though half the Greek world claims him—the strongest contenders are probably Chios and Smyrna. But he certainly didn't come from Syria, where few if any Greeks were living when his poems were written.

At some point probably rather early in his life, Meleager began writing epigrams. He must have known the work of the important Hellenistic poets, certainly of Asclepiades and Callimachus, who served as his most significant models. For just as the Hellenistic poets wrote variations on the work of their contemporaries, so Meleager, who may not have *had* contemporaries to emulate, sought model epigrams in the published poetry of his predecessors. Meleager was conscious of the relationship between his poetry and that of earlier authors, since when he assembled the *Garland* he placed poems on similar themes together, distributing his own poems among those of Asclepiades, Callimachus, and other poets, often putting his poems at the end as if to cap the preceding epigrams. For example, Meleager seems to have placed Callimachus's epigram about Kleonikos (XXVII) just before his own poem about Damis (IX); both describe a lovesick man wasting away after meeting eyes with a good-looking adolescent. Asclepiades VII is followed directly by Meleager VIII in the *Greek Anthology* and probably also in the *Garland,* and both poems are about the poet pining away from love and asking for release. I point out additional examples in the notes. Meleager used the organization of his collection to make clear his relationship to his predecessors, highlighting his own achievement as well as his affinity with the acknowledged masters of the genre.

Meleager wrote poems within the Hellenistic tradition of epigram, including epitaphs (I) and dedications (II and XXX). It is not, however, on these poems that his reputation rests, but rather on his delightful love epigrams, which make up the great majority of his surviving work and most of the rest of this chapter. Meleager tells us (in IV) that his first love was for the adolescent boy Myiskos, and we have eleven poems—perhaps among Meleager's earliest—addressed to Myiskos and preserved in the *Greek Anthology*. Together with his other love poems to young men, they show an especially strong influence of Asclepiades and Callimachus.

At some later time in his life, Meleager began to write love poetry addressed to women as well; these writings were also influenced by earlier Hellenistic poets though in ways that are often less obvious. He must have continued to write poems to women for much of the rest of his life, since his epigrams addressed to a woman he calls Phanion were written in Kos (see GP 66, *AP* 12.53), where he says he spent his old age. In one of his poems (XV) he appears to make a definite break, casting the boys aside with "I'm fond of female love." We should not take this declaration too literally, however, since two poems written in praise of the young man he calls Praxiteles (GP 110 and 111, *AP* 12.56 and 12.57) were written in Kos long after the Myiskos poems.

Though the influence of Meleager's predecessors is pervasive in his verse, his love poetry has its own distinctive character. The poems of Asclepiades and Callimachus are original and witty but seem detached. Love is a game, and there is seldom any expression of affection. Many of Meleager's love poems are like this too, but in some he communicates a deeper feeling largely foreign to the work of earlier poets. We sense in XIII the poet's longing for his dream of love, in XVIII the ripeness and beauty of young Zenophila, in XX the poet's feeling of otherness and almost overwhelming desire of possession, and in XXII his hope for communion of his soul with his beloved. These are not sentiments we ordinarily associate with Hellenistic poets.

Many critics have faulted Meleager for insincerity and frivolity. Carl

Radinger complained that Meleager's various lovers seem to blend into one another, that his verse gives the impression of a divertissement not based on actual experience. Others have argued that his epigrams cannot be heartfelt, because he wrote poems to such a large number of lovers. How could anyone care so much for so many? We can of course never know whether Meleager actually slept with all of the boys and women he mentions in his poems, or even if all of these lovers existed; but if he did go to bed with all of them, few now would take him to task. One recent survey claims that American men have a median of seven lovers over the course of their lives, and British men almost twice that number. Meleager was a wealthy member of the Greek upper class, and there is no indication in his poems that he ever married (as we find in the poetry of Philodemos; see his epigrams XV–XVIII and notes). To have (or at least to *claim* to have) so many lovers may have been common and expected.

Some critics also complain that Meleager's verse is sentimental and bombastic, but these criticisms are usually directed at his worst poems. The best are beautifully written, concise and felicitous of expression; moreover, they are as passionate and sensual as anything in Hellenistic verse. They remind us more of Shakespeare's sonnets than of other Hellenistic love poetry. Meleager might have read his poems to a mistress and received (at a minimum) a smile of appreciation—something that can be said only rarely of the love poems of his predecessors.

That is not to say, however, that Meleager was a better poet. When in the *Garland* he put his own epigrams next to those of earlier poets, he implicitly invited readers to make the comparison. Many who have done so have given Meleager second prize. As the nineteenth-century French critic Sainte-Beuve observed, Meleager ranks below the great poets of the third century; but among poets of the second order, he is at the top of the list. We are reminded of Martial, who wished to be second only to Catullus. To be second to poets like Asclepiades and Callimachus is not so bad. Meleager would probably have been pleased.

I

"Tyre was my nurse, but Gádara was the town
Where I was born, where Greeks had settled down
In Syria. I was Eukrátes' son,
The poet Meleáger, having first run
With my Menippean *Graces* a close race.
If I am Syrian, so what? One place,
The world, we all call fatherland, my friend,
And mortals from one Chaos all descend."
These things on tablets I inscribed before
My tomb, an old man, neighbor of death's door.
Come wish my garrulous old age good cheer,
And may you prattle too when death is near.

II

Oh locust, oh deceiver of desire,
Oh sleep's persuader, chirping with your wing,
For me, oh nature's mimic of the lyre,
Oh rustic Muse, some song of yearning sing
By striking vocal wings with your dear feet,
So you might weave a sound upon the air
To cure my pain, a melody to cheat
This love, and rescue me from sleepless care.
At dawn I'll give you green leek when you've sung,
And dewy morsels portioned for your tongue.

III

As a woman, Aphrodite throws a fire
Of mania for girls; but of desire
For boys, there Cupid holds the reins. And so,
    Whither shall I go?
      To which one?
   The mother or the son?

Yet even Aphrodite, I surmise,
Would say her cocky kid would win first prize.

IV

Myḯskos, with his eyes as from a bow,
Shot me, whose breast had never felt love's blow,
And cried, "I've got His Majesty, look now!
The impudence that sat upon his brow
Of sceptered wisdom with my feet I tread!"
Then barely breathing, this to him I said:
"My dear boy, why does this astonish you?
Down from Olympus Cupid brought Zeus too."

V

"The die is cast! Light torches! I shall go."
Look here, such recklessness! And you are so
    Dead drunk with wine! If you've been drinking,
    What deep thought can you be thinking?
    "I shall revel, I shall revel!" Heart,
    Where are you turning? "Is there part
    Of love that logic can lay bare?
    Light torches quickly!" But then, where
    Is your past wont to syllogize?
    "Let my great effort to be wise
Be cast aside. I've just one thing to say:
Even from Zeus Love took the will away."

VI

One loveliness is everything to me,
One thing alone my greedy eyes can see,
    Myḯskos; to all else I'm blind,
    Whatever comes into my mind
Is him. Or do my flattering eyes alight
On only what would give my heart delight?

VII

My life is moored to you, in you
    What soul I've left; I vow
By eyes that speak, boy, even to
    The deaf, by your bright brow,

If overcast the look you throw,
    Then winter do I see,
But if your glance good cheer would show,
    Then sweet spring blooms for me.

VIII

A winter wind of tear-sweet love for you,
Myḯskos, brings me, carried off by too
    Much reveling. A mighty sigh
    Of longing storms across the sky;
But to your sheltered harbor welcome me,
A sailor sailing Aphrodite's sea.

IX

Already sweet dawn's come, but in between
    The court and front door Dámis lies,
    Unhappy man, and sleepless sighs
Away the breath he's left still, having seen
Now Heraclitus. He stood in the glance
    Of that one's eyes into his own,
    Like wax that on live coal was thrown.
But Dámis, come, sad victim of mischance,
Wake up, a wound of love have even I,
And adding to your tears I also cry.

X

If Cupid had no wings or bow
    Or quiver, and no fire

Of arrows, burning with the blow
   Of longing and desire,
I swear that you would never guess
   Which of the two was he,
Or from the shape and comeliness
   Which one would Zoilos be.

XI

Still in his mother's lap a child at play,
With knucklebones Love bet my life away.

XII

The south wind, blowing fair to sailors, stole
Andrágathos from me, half of my soul.
Oh three times happy are the ships, and three
Times fortunate the breakers of the sea,
But four times glad the wind that boys convey!
Oh would I were a dolphin and could lay
Him ferried on my shoulders, so that he
Could look on Rhodes, so sweet for boys to see!

XIII

Cupid brought a pleasant dream to me,
A boy of eighteen laughing winsomely,
In his short cloak still; I round his soft skin
Beneath the covers pressed my chest, drew in
False hope. Still now, the longing that I keep
Of this remembrance warms me, I have sleep
About my eyes forever on patrol
To find this wingéd shade. Oh lovesick soul,
Stop even in your dreams at last to feel
Vain heat for visions, lovely but unreal!

XIV

Once fair was Heraclitus, new,
    But now a past-date rind
Of leather ass declares war to
    Those mounting from behind.

Polyxenídes, these things knowing,
    Don't so proudly prance,
For Nemesis is also growing
    In your underpants.

XV

No longer "lovely Théron" do I write,
Nor "lovely Apollódotus," once who
    Before so fiery bright,
    Is now burnt residue.

I'm fond of female love. Let others bore
Down homophilic holes with hairy coats;
    This now can be the chore
    Of shepherds who mount goats.

XVI

Oh Dawn, no friend of love, why do you come
So slowly to the heavens, when now some
New lover warms himself in Demó's bed?
But when I had her in my arms instead,
How quickly you stood near, as if to throw
A light on me that gloried in my woe.

XVII

How sweetly, Zenophíla, your harp sings,
By Pan, how sweetly can you strike the strings!
Where do I flee?
In every place
Are Cupids circling me,
They leave no breathing space.
Your shape, your Muse, your charm, your . . . which to say?
I'm burning with desire in every way.

XVIII

Already now white violets are in flower,
Narcissus too blooms, basking in rain's shower,
And lilies, haunting mountains; but the rose
Of sweet seduction, Zenophíla, glows
In ripeness and has come to flower too
Among the flowers, friend of love. Why do
You laugh, oh meadows, with leaves idly gay?
Your fragrant garlands bow beneath her sway.

XIX

Bold siphons of the blood of men,
Two-wingéd buzzing fiends of night,
Spare little Zenophíla when
She sleeps in quiet. Look here! Bite

My own limbs, eat my flesh I pray,
Mosquitoes, merciless! But why
Stupidities do I still say?
For even wild beasts like to lie

Warmed in soft flesh. But come now, show
More caution, evil creatures, and
Be not so reckless, or you'll know
The power of a jealous hand.

XX

You slumber, Zenophíla, lovely lass.
Would that upon your eyes I now could pass
As Sleep but without wings, so that the god,
Whose spell can even Zeus's eyelids nod,
Would not so often come, but I alone
Would be the one to have you for my own.

XXI

Fleet messenger, mosquito, fly
Along to Zenophíla's ear; there may
You reach its tip and whisper, and this say:
"Without a wink he's made to lie

Awaiting you; you sleep, and you've
Forgotten those who love you." Fly now, go,
Friend of the Muses! But speak softly, so
Her lover doesn't wake, don't move

Against me his pained jealousies.
And if you bring her, I shall have you wear
A lion's skin, and in your hand you'll bear
A cudgel just like Hercules.

XXII

The cup delights in pleasure, telling how
It touches Zenophíla's babbling lip.
Oh lucky! With her lips on mine, would now
That she could drink my soul up in one sip!

XXIII

I keep a Cupid who plays ball, and he
Takes this heart that goes up and down in me,
And throws it, Heliodóra, off to you.
Have Cupid as your playmate; if you do
Not throw my heart back, but cast it aside,
   Breaking the rule
  , We learn in school,
This wanton outrage he will not abide.

XXIV

Why do you land, oh floral-feeding bee,
On Heliodóra's skin, and spring buds flee?
   Is it to tell that she the sting
   Of love both sweet and sharp can bring,
   Forever bitter to the heart?
   Yes, this I think you do impart.
Go back to blooms, oh lover's friend, we know
Your news already, knew it long ago!

XXV

She's taken! Who so brutal, who so great
Brings war to Love? Light torches, quick! But wait,
That's Heliodóra's footfall I discern.
Oh heart, back to my chest again return!

XXVI

Give her, Dorkás, this message; say
It two times, and then, see, a third,
And run! Do not, Dorkás, delay,
But fly off! Wait, another word,

Dorkás, a word. Dorkás, where do
You hurry to before you know
The whole? To what I just told you
Not long ago, add this . . . although . . .

What nonsense! Don't tell anything!
It's just that—no, the whole thing say!
Why send you? Come, Dorkás, I'll bring
You with me. Look, I'll lead the way!

XXVII

I know, don't think that you can hide;
Don't call down gods, I've found you out.
That's what it was, that's it! You swore and lied,
But now I've learned what it was all about.

Alone you slept? She keeps on too,
"Alone," still now "alone" to say!
That handsome Kléon, didn't he with you . . . ?
Or if not him . . . ? Why threaten? Go away,

Base vermin of my bed, quick, go!
But wait . . . a favor, a delight
I'll give you, wanting to see him, I know:
Stay here like this a captive, tied up tight!

XXVIII

I know you swore to me in vain: your hair,
    In perfume steeped not long ago,
    Betrays your lust, your eyelids show
You're sleepless, see, they droop! Your tresses bear

The thread that held your garland, tightly bound.
    Your curls have recently been rent
    And rumpled in your merriment,
You drag your drunken, tottering limbs around.

Go fuck off, woman anyone can screw!
    The harp, your friend in merrymaking,
    And the clatter of hand-quaking
Castanets, are surely calling you!

XXIX

Oh sacred night and oil lamp, when we two
Made vows, we took no witnesses but you.
He swore he'd love me, and I gave my oath
I'd never leave him, joint pledge from us both.
    But he says these words we have sworn
      On water now are born,
    And you, lamp, see in his embrace
      Another in my place.

XXX

Oh stars, my roaming festive lyre, and night,
Oh moon, to lovers spreading your fair light,
Shall I see her by lamp lamenting, still
In bed awake, that profligate? Or will
She have someone? Consumed by tears, I lay
These wreaths as suppliants on her doorway,
And placing an inscription near them, write
This one thing: "Meleager, acolyte
Of your carousing, hung for you above,
Oh Aphrodite, these spoils of his love."

EXPLANATORY NOTES

I (GP 2, AP 7.417)

Meleager put several epitaphs in the *Garland,* including at least four self-epitaphs in the tradition of Callimachus V. These poems give the name "Meleager" and provide much of our information about the poet's life. A poem containing the name of the poet was often used as a *sphragis* or "seal" to indicate authorship of a poetry collection (see Asclepiades XX), and a poem like this might have been placed as the concluding poem in a book. Meleager may have composed several self-epitaphs throughout his life for different collections of poetry. With the phrase "having first run / With my Menippean *Graces* a close race," Meleager appears to be saying that he first entered a literary competition with his *Charites* or *Graces*. That he doesn't mention a victory suggests that he probably didn't win. Chaos in Hesiod's *Theogony* was a dark chasm that existed at the very beginning of the universe; from it, Blackness and dark Night were born. Meleager describes his old age as *lalios,* which is difficult to translate into English. The basic meaning of *lalios* or *lalos* is "talkative," but it often means something closer to "garrulous" or "prattling." When Meleager uses this word of a woman (as in XXII), it is clearly a term of approbation and is impossible to render adequately in English. Our words are all either neutral or derogatory, perhaps reflecting a cultural difference. The Greeks apparently found talkative women attractive, whereas the English are better known for their admiration of discretion and reticence.

II (GP 12; AP 7.195)

This is a love poem in the form of a prayer. It is addressed to an *akris* as if to a god; *akris* can mean cricket in Greek but here more likely means locust or field grasshopper, as in Anyte IX and Leonidas X. A cricket makes its song by rubbing its forewings together, whereas a locust strikes its hind limb against the edge of its forewing, much as Meleager describes in the poem. As in a hymn to a god, the poem asks the "rustic Muse" for a benefaction in the form of a song, and in return he promises some sort of favor, here food offerings. The poem may have been used at the beginning of a section of love epigrams; after asking the locust to sing its songs, the poet may then have sung his own. Although Hellenistic poets had previously written epitaphs for pet insects, Meleager reinvents this theme as amatory verse. The result is sentimental, but I confess a weakness for it.

III (GP 18, AP 12.86)

Meleager wrote love poems for boys and women, and poems of both kinds were combined together in his *Garland* though later separated by Cephalas when the *Greek Anthology* was assembled. This poem is clearly programmatic and may have introduced a sequence of poems about boy lovers; I have used it in this way as well. Meleager's division of love into spheres controlled by Eros (Cupid) and Aphrodite (Venus) is a clever conceit but nothing more. Cupid is represented as a god of love for women in some of his other epigrams (e.g., XVII, XXIII).

IV (GP 103, AP 12.101)

I have put the epigrams for boys before those for women and this epigram at the beginning, since Meleager clearly identifies Myiskos as his first love. In a poem I haven't translated (GP 78, *AP* 12.256), Meleager includes Myiskos in a circle of boys in Tyre to whom he says he was attracted, and this suggests that Meleager remained in Tyre at least through his adolescence and early manhood. In the present poem, Myiskos claims to have overcome the "impudence" of Meleager's "sceptered wisdom." We are meant to imagine the poet as a studious and dutiful young man, immersed in philosophy and displaying what the Greeks called *sophrosyne* ("moderation" or "self-control"), but now vanquished by first love. In the *Greek Anthology* this epigram appears only a few poems after Posidippus XI, in which the poet claims that his study of books has protected him from love's passion. Meleager says this hasn't worked as well for him, but we probably should not take either poet at his word. This poem provided the model for the beginning of the first poem in the first book of love elegies by the Latin poet Propertius.

V (GP 19, AP 12.117)

This epigram describes more explicitly than IV the struggle over love between the poet's heart and his intellect. In addition to its similar theme, it has a similar last line. The poem takes the form of a dialogue that the heart begins, declaring that it is about to leave to go reveling. The poet's intellect admonishes the heart not to make such a rash decision when heavy with wine. The heart doesn't even bother to answer but merely repeats its determination. The intellect then reminds the heart of the poet's earlier study of philosophy, but the heart firmly disavows the pursuit of wisdom in favor of love. Like IV, this epigram has clear affinities with Posidippus XI as well as XII, but in Posidippus we have a better sense of a contest. Meleager seems to give up rather easily.

VI – VIII *(GP 104, AP 12.106; GP 108, AP 12.159; and GP 109, AP 12.167)*

These three epigrams are conventional in theme, but it would be uncharitable of us two thousand years later to recount the number of times love poets have written "you are my everything." It is doubtful that this sentiment was fresh even for Meleager, though so little of ancient lyric has survived that it is difficult for us now to be sure. These poems are nevertheless affecting, though they require some suspension of the critical faculty. But then, first love is like that.

IX *(GP 92, AP 12.72)*

Heraclitus is also mentioned by Meleager in *AP* 12.256 as one of the boys of Tyre, so this poem probably dates from the same period as the Myiskos poems. It is an interesting epigram for its echoes of the love poetry of Asclepiades and Callimachus. Asclepiades in XVII says "I melt with desire / Like wax by the fire" and Meleager "Like wax that on live coal was thrown"; Callimachus writes in XXVII "You looked, poor man, with both your eyes" and Meleager "in the glance / Of that one's eyes into his own." Variation of the themes of other poets was standard practice in third-century Greece; like any poet learning his craft, Meleager turned to earlier poets whose work he particularly admired.

X *(GP 89, AP 12.76)*

This poem has clear affinities with Asclepiades XIX, similar not only in its subject matter but also in much of its wording. Meleager's poem is placed just after Asclepiades' poem in the *Greek Anthology* and they were probably also adjacent in the *Garland*. In this way the reader could notice that in Asclepiades XIX the boy would be mistaken for Cupid if the boy had wings and a bow, whereas in Meleager X it is just the opposite: Cupid would be mistaken for the boy if the god *lacked* his usual paraphernalia.

XI *(GP 15, AP 12.47)*

This poem is placed in the *Greek Anthology* directly after Asclepiades VI, with which it shares similar wording and the same image of Cupid (Love) playing a game of chance with the life of the poet. I have placed it among the poems about boys, since this is where Cephalas seems to have put it when he divided up the love poems according to the sex of the love object, but it could equally well have been written about women or about love for both sexes.

XII *(GP 81, AP 12.52)*

This poem, too, may have been written in Tyre, since a south wind (blowing from south to north) would have been favorable for a boat sailing to Rhodes from Tyre but not from Kos. The phrase "half of my soul" comes from Callimachus XXII. The progression "three," "three," "but four" is Homeric. In *Odyssey* 21.125–29, for example, when Telemachus tries to string the great bow that Ulysses later aims at the suitors, Homer writes: "Three times he made it quiver in his eagerness to draw it, and three times he relaxed his effort, though hoping in his heart to string the bow and shoot an arrow through the iron. And now a fourth time he would have succeeded as he drew up the string with effort, but Ulysses nodded in dissent and checked his zeal." The image of a dolphin carrying the boy across the sea may be taken in part from a story told by the fifth-century BCE Greek historian Herodotus about the famous musician Arion. Threatened with death by thieving sailors aboard ship, Arion took up his lyre, sang his most famous song, and then threw himself into the sea, where he was picked up by a presumably appreciative dolphin who carried him to shore.

XIII *(GP 117, AP 12.125)*

There is in this original epigram a vividness unlike anything in earlier Hellenistic love poetry, especially in the phrase "I have sleep / About my eyes forever on patrol / To find this wingéd shade." The poem is Meleager at his best, less dependent on Asclepiades or Callimachus and in a direct line to Catullus and Latin love elegy. We shall discover more poems like this when we turn from the boys to Meleager's women.

XIV (GP 90, AP 12.33)

Greek pederasty normally occurred between an older *erastes* and an adolescent boy, called an *eromenos,* who was usually between the ages of twelve and eighteen. The boy was thought to be too old and no longer attractive once he had sprouted body hair or his beard had become thick. Smooth skin would seem also to have been a *sine qua non.* Meleager describes the bottom of Heraclitus as a *derris,* a leather covering. This word can also mean a screen of hide hung before a fortification to deaden the blow of an enemy's missile. The pun is untranslatable. Nemesis is the goddess of retribution or divine wrath, who generally directed her anger against those who had succumbed to hubris and had become insolent or overbearing. The poem is a warning to Polyxenides not to exult over the ill fortune of Heraclitus, since in time his own *gluteus maximus* will suffer a similar fate.

XV (GP 94, AP 12.41)

This indelicate poem, like III, is programmatic and was probably used by Meleager to introduce a series of epigrams about heterosexual love. I have used it in this way as well: all of the remaining poems in this chapter are about women. Theron is mentioned by Meleager as one of the boys of Tyre, so this poem is likely to date from the same era as the Myiskos epigrams. It is often mistranslated. What the poem says literally is "let the *piesma* of hairy-holed sexual passives be the concern of shepherds who are goat-mounters." The word *piesma* is sometimes translated to mean "hugging," a sense it is unlikely to take. A better translation is "pushing," since *piesma* comes from the verb *piezo,* to "squeeze" or "press tight." The rest of the poem indicates that Meleager had something more than "hugging" in mind.

XVI (GP 28, AP 5.173)

Just as he names Myiskos and other boys and men repeatedly in his poems, so Meleager uses the name of the same woman in more than one poem, something his predecessors appear to have done much less frequently. It is possible that the names he used in every case referred to real people, as Gow and Page suggested, though it is equally possible that these names were made up and that the characters in his poems are fictional composites. What is clear, however, is that the poet presents the women in his poetry as distinct individuals; by using names to link together poems of a similar nature, almost in the form of a narrative, he provided the model later followed by Latin love elegy. The present poem is one of two that Meleager wrote about dawn seeming to come too early, both of which mention the woman Demo. The poet does not blame Demo for her attentions to another lover but instead accuses dawn of arriving sooner for the poet than for the other man. Doesn't dawn on a bright sunny morning give pleasure to everyone? No, Meleager says, not to those whose time for making love ends when morning begins.

XVII – XXII (GP 29, AP 5.139; GP 31, AP 5.144; GP 33, AP 5.151; GP 36, AP 5.174; GP 34, AP 5.152; and GP 35, AP 5.171)

These six poems, drawn from the twelve in the *Garland* addressed to Meleager's mistress Zenophila, are among his best. They vary in mood from the excited desperation of XVII to the charming sentimentality of XVIII and quiet ardor of XX. The two mosquito poems (XIX and XXI) are clever and apparently original; for the lion's skin and cudgel of Hercules (XXI), see the note to Callimachus XVIII.

XXIII (GP 53, AP 5.214)

Heliodora is another of the women Meleager names in several of his poems. The conceit of Cupid playing ball with a lover comes from the sixth-century BCE Greek poet Anacreon, but Meleager makes the ball the lover's heart. The rest seems a bit muddled. We can understand what it might mean for Cupid to throw the poet's heart to Heliodora and to have her catch it. But why would he want her to continue the game and throw his heart back? The "school" mentioned in the poem is the *palaistra*— originally a place for wrestling and boxing, which was usually associated with a gymnasium, a building where boys and young men took physical exercise and could also receive intellectual instruction.

XXIV and XXV (GP 50, AP 5.163 and GP 55, AP 12.147)

Two more love poems to Heliodora, original in theme and elegant in execution. The notion in XXIV that love is bittersweet goes back in Greek literature as far as Sappho (see note to Asclepiades XV), but Meleager has given it a new twist. Meleager XXV is remarkable for its drama; there is nothing quite like it elsewhere in Greek epigram. Meleager wakes up in the middle of the night and no longer finds Heliodora next to him. In his panic he imagines that someone has come and taken her, but he is suddenly reassured when he hears her footfall.

XXVI and XXVII (GP 71, AP 5.182 and GP 72, AP 5.184)

These two poems are based on the tradition of Greek mimes: dramatic poems comparatively short and spoken (unlike modern mime), with a small group of characters—sometimes only one. Mimes were written in verse but mimicked ordinary speech and emphasized character development rather than plot. In these two poems of Meleager, there is only a single speaker, whose manner of speech—short, interrupted sentences that mix indicative, interrogative, and imperative moods—is intended to convey the spontaneity of a man actually talking. Both poems are about a woman, and Henri Ouvré thought that they were written as a pair: in the first, the poet is unable to decide whether he should look the other way or confront the woman; by the second, he has made up his mind and does confront her. But though the second of the poems is clearly about a woman's perceived infidelities, nothing is clear about the first. We keep expecting the poem to tell us what message Dorkas is to give, what "whole" he is going to say, but we reach the end of the poem knowing little more than we did at the beginning. What we learn instead is the emotional state of the man in the poem, who vacillates between two extremes, each proclaimed with the greatest vehemence. The man in the second poem also expresses himself in the strongest terms; his only hesitation comes at the conclusion, when instead of sending the woman away he suddenly decides to tie her up. He is however quite different in character from the person in the first epigram, and the contrast was probably intentional. Dorkas may have been the name of a slave; it is also the name of a go-between in another of Meleager's poems (GP 58, *AP* 5.187).

XXVIII (GP 70, AP 5.175)

Another poem about an unfaithful woman and nearly identical in theme to XXVII, but much less like mime. The sentences are longer with many fewer independent clauses, and the elaborate organization of the syntax and carefully chosen vocabulary give the impression of a man who has thought long and hard about his grievances and has reached a breaking point.

XXIX (GP 69, AP 5.8)

This next epigram turns the tables on the previous two and gives us a woman complaining about the faithlessness of a man. It is based in part on Asclepiades XV, in which a woman also speaks and complains about her lover, but it has clear affinities as well with a poem by Callimachus about a jilted girl (GP 11, *AP* 5.6). I have followed Gow and Page and placed this poem among those of Meleager, though it is sometimes attributed to Philodemos, and there is no certain way of deciding which of the two (if either) actually wrote the poem. The image of the words of a faithless lover written and carried away by water is at least as old as Sophocles and was also used by the Latin poet Catullus in one of his most famous poems (70):

My woman says there's no one she'd prefer
  To marry more than me,
Not even if she's asked by Jupiter.

She says this, but the words that women declare
  To eager lovers should be
Written on rushing water and in the air.

XXX (GP 73, AP 5.191)

Garlands are placed on the door of a beloved in Asclepiades XIII, but in Meleager the garlands are suppliants, formally to the goddess of love but also by implication to the woman. The garlands are accompanied by an inscription, which in the Greek (and in my translation) curiously begins in midline and does not satisfy the metrical requirements of an independent poem. Kathryn Gutzwiller (in *Poetic Garlands*) has suggested that XXX may have been placed by Meleager at the end of a sequence of love epigrams, first because it has Meleager's name as a *sphragis* or "seal," and second because the act of writing an epigram on a garland in the poem may have been intended to symbolize the placing of epigrams within the *Garland* of poetry. The word *skyla* or "spoils" in the last line is borrowed directly from actual dedication inscriptions. Meleager calls himself Aphrodite's *mystes,* which I have translated as "acolyte"; it is the Greek word for someone who has been initiated into a god's mystery rites.

CHAPTER NINE

Philodemos

Nearly 150 years after the appearance of Meleager's *Garland,* a second anthology of epigrams was assembled by the poet Philip of Thessalonica, just before or during the reign of the Roman emperor Nero. Of all the poets Philip included I have selected only one, who is not only the best of the poets of this second *Garland* but also one of the very finest of all the Greek composers of epigrams. Philodemos was born around 110 BCE, about fifty years after Meleager in the same city of Gadara in Palestine. Like Meleager he left Gadara at an early age, probably driven out with his family by the incessant warfare between Greek and Jewish armies.

He is then known to have made his way to Athens, where he studied with the head of the Epicurean school of philosophy, Zenon (or Zeno) of Sidon, whose lectures Cicero also attended in 79–78 BCE.

Like many Greek artists and intellectuals, Philodemos eventually went to Italy. We do not know when he arrived or how he got there, but by 55 BCE, when Philodemos was in his early to mid-fifties, he was already well-known in Rome. We know this because Cicero delivered a speech in 55 BCE in the Senate against a political enemy, L. Calpurnius Piso Caesoninus, who was the father-in-law of Julius Caesar. In this speech, which Cicero later published, he describes a "certain Greek" who was practically living with Piso—an Epicurean philosopher who wrote poetry "so merry, so well-composed, and so elegant that nothing could be more quick-witted and clever." That Greek philosopher and poet was Philodemos, who by this time had found his place in Roman society. In epigram XIX, Philodemos invites Piso to dinner to celebrate the feast of Epicurus, combining in one poem evidence for Philodemos as poet and Epicurean philosopher and for Piso as his friend and eventual patron.

Though some of Philodemos's poetry survived in the second *Garland,* his philosophical works were entirely lost until the middle of the eighteenth century, when a building now called the Villa of the Papyri was discovered in Herculaneum, a town on the coast of Italy just south of Naples. Herculaneum, like Pompeii, was entirely buried in ash by the eruption of Vesuvius in 79 CE. In addition to many statues and wall paintings in this villa, which clearly indicated its ownership by a prominent family, the excavators discovered about a thousand book scrolls, some in a library and some in carrying boxes for transporting them to safety. Carbonized but in many cases at least partially legible, the scrolls consist mostly of Greek texts of Epicurean philosophy, including many works by Philodemos on poetry, rhetoric, music, ethics, theology, and the history of philosophy, which may have been in part the texts of his lectures. One of these books, *On the Good King According to Homer,* is dedicated to Piso, and many scholars now believe that the Villa of the Papyri originally belonged to Piso, who died more than a hundred years before the eruption. The house and its books may then have remained in Piso's family until they were buried by the ash and mud of Vesuvius.

From these books and from passages in Cicero and other authors, we can put together some notion of the life of Philodemos after his arrival in Italy until his death, perhaps not long after 40 BCE. Philodemos appears to have spent most of his time in the region around Naples, which was then the center of the teaching of Epicurean philosophy in Italy. We should picture him sitting with friends on quiet evenings, eating and drinking in moderation as they discussed philosophy, perhaps in the company of women with similar interests. During the day, Philodemos would have written his philosophy books and, every now and then, a poem; he would also have taught the young, giving lectures on the theory of poetic composition and on Epicurean ethics and metaphysics. His friends included not just fellow Epicurean philosophers and upper-class Romans like Piso but also many of the most important names in Roman literature. In one of the books found at Herculaneum, Philodemos addresses Virgil by name, as well as Quintilius Varus, an admired critic and friend of Horace; the poet L. Varius Rufus, who wrote *On Death,* an epic poem known to us from a few fragments; and Plotius Tucca, who together with Varius Rufus prepared the *Aeneid* for publication after Virgil's untimely death. All these men were also friends of Horace. Horace was familiar with Philodemos's poetry (see notes to V and VII), but we do not know if the two actually met, since Horace may have been too young to have made the trip from Rome to Naples before the philosopher died.

There may also be a reference to Philodemos in the poetry of Catullus. In poem 47 Catullus complains of the treatment of two of his friends who had been overseas in the service of Piso, presumably in Macedonia. Catullus insults Piso by calling him a "circumcised Priapus" and upbraids him for doing nothing for Catullus's friends but preferring instead the company of two other men, Porcius and Socration. Though Porcius is a perfectly good Latin patrician name, Socration, "little Socrates," is Greek and may have been a nickname. Since Philodemos in several epigrams refers to a woman he says he courted and married as "Xanthippe" (see

XIV–XVIII and notes), which was the name of Socrates' wife, Socration may very well have been Philodemos's nickname, used with contempt by Catullus in this poem but perhaps with affection by Philodemos's friends and students.

One of the great puzzles of Philodemos's life and work is how we are to reconcile his witty and off-color poetry with his ascetic philosophy. Epicurus says in his famous letter to Menoeceus that "it is not an unbroken succession of drinking bouts and revelry, not sexual lust, not the enjoyment of fish and other delicacies that make a pleasant life, but sober reasoning, the investigation of the grounds of every choice and avoidance, and the banishing of those beliefs that cause the greatest disturbance of the soul." Philodemos seems to have shared this view (see XIX and note), but the majority of the epigrams are full of "drinking bouts and revelry," not to mention "sexual lust"; cleverly phrased and carefully constructed, they are brimming with life. The prose writings of Philodemos by comparison seem dour and plodding.

One possibility is that Philodemos wrote most of his epigrams as a young man before becoming established as an Epicurean philosopher. In two of his poems (XV and XVI), he says that his gray hair proclaims the "age of wisdom," and he rejects his former dissolute life in favor of moderation and sobriety. A turning point may have been his marriage to Xanthippe, the woman Philodemos calls the "flourish" ending his "insanity" (XVI). The difficulty with this proposal, however plausible, is that we have no evidence of any kind for the dating of the poems, nor are we permitted to assume that the voice of a poem is the poet's own. Epigram V calls for a girl who is accessible and doesn't cost much, whereas II says just the opposite: "I go / For anything that's under lock and key." While it is possible that Philodemos changed his mind about women, it may be more useful to recall that easy and difficult women were common subjects of Greek and Latin poetry beginning at least with Callimachus XX, and that Philodemos wrote two poems and perhaps more on this theme, deliberately adopting different points of view. Some of Philodemos's epigrams may very well be autobiographical, XIX in particular, but many cannot be. The difficulty is that we do not know which are which.

It may be more illuminating to put Philodemos's life to one side and to consider instead how similar his poetic program was to that of Asclepiades. Both poets display love in much of its variety, though for Philodemos only between men and women. Philodemos gives us lovers of all ages, from virgins (II, VII) to the elderly (VIII, XX). We meet streetwalkers (XIII), adulterers both male (IV) and female (XI), and happy couples (VI), in one case even married (XVIII). The tone of the poems also resembles that of Asclepiades: clever and lighthearted, with little that could be called heartfelt. In this respect Philodemos resembles the poets of the third century much more than he does his near-contemporary Meleager.

Cicero says that Philodemos and Piso were up to their necks in wine-soaked debauchery, and that the epigrams are a record of these orgies. This is of course possible, but it is unwise to take Cicero at his word when he is attacking an enemy. It seems just as likely that many of these poems were written by a sex-starved young man in a garret in Athens long before he ever met Piso. Was Xanthippe really the poet's wife? Or did Philodemos invent her to provide a narrative of his transition from amorous poet to serious philosopher? The written record does not permit us to resolve these questions with any confidence.

We can nevertheless be certain that Philodemos was one of the most interesting men of the late Roman Republic, a friend and probably teacher of some of the most important figures in Latin literature, and one of the very best poets of Greek epigrams. There is a sense in which the Greek love epigram in the tradition of Asclepiades, Callimachus, and Meleager died with Philodemos. Although Greek poets continued to write epigrams on love, none was ever again as good. Love poetry became instead the province of Latin poets—of Catullus, Propertius, and Ovid. Greek love poets continued to grind out pale imitations of their predecessors, but of far greater interest are men like Lucillius who took Greek epigrammatic poetry in a quite different direction, as we shall see in the final chapter.

I

My heart knows my past tears and jealousy,
And warns me Heliodóra's love to flee,
But I've no strength to do what it would say.
It's shameless: warns me, then loves anyway.

II

Demó is killing me, and Thérmion too;
Demó's a virgin, Thérmion I pay;
I fondle one, the other's still taboo.
By Aphrodite, which one should I say
Is more desirable? I'll say Demó,
The maiden, since availability
Is not what I am fond of, but I go
For anything that's under lock and key.

III

I fell in love once with Demó, who came
From Paphos—big surprise! Then one whose name
Was yet a second time Demó, and who
Was Samian—no wonder! With a new
Demó from Nysa, this was now no joke.
A fourth one came from Argos. The Fates spoke
And named me Philodemos, I suppose
To have hot longing always for Demós.

IV

When on the breasts of Kýdilla I lay,
Daring to go at dusk or in the day,
I stepped along a precipice, I know
I risk my life each time these dice I throw.
But what's the use? For when Love draws me near,
He's always bold without a dream of fear.

V

When what's-his-name fucks once with you-know-who,
He pays five talents, shivering with fear;
She isn't even pretty. I can screw
Twelve times with Lysiánassa, a mere
Five drachmas pay, and in addition we
Don't have to hide, and she's much better made.
So either I'm completely mad, or he
Should end with his balls cut off by a blade.

VI

Nocturnal two-horned Moon, come cast your light,
You, who love reveling throughout the night,
Fall down through lattice windows, your beams spill
On golden-haired Kallístion. Ill-will
Comes not to you, a goddess, when you throw
Your glance on what two lovers do; I know
You're glad for this girl and for me, since you
Once fell in love with Endymíon too.

VII

A calyx still your summer fruit encases,
Your grapes aren't dark with early maiden graces,
But youthful Cupids sharpen arrows, and
Already, Lysidíkë, a firebrand
   Is hidden somewhere,
   Smoke fills the air.
The arrow's not yet on the string. Let's flee!
A prophet, I, of great flame soon to be.

VIII

Through sixty summers has the sun progressed,
    But Charitó's long hair stays black,
    Her breasts, though they be bare and lack
Supporting bands that circle round her chest,

Are little marble cones; her skin, unlined,
    Can still ambrosia exude,
    Persuading still to be pursued
In every way, with charms of every kind.

So, lovers, all of you who have no fears
    Of passion to a frenzy stirred,
    Come hither and be not deterred,
Unmindful of the decade of her years.

IX

Philaínion is small and dark, but she
Has more curls than the fronds of celery;
Her skin is softer than a young bird's feather;
Her voice is magical, more altogether
Than Aphrodite's girdle it entices;
She offers all, oblivious of prices.
May I love such a one as she, until
I find another, who's more perfect still.

X

You weep, talk pitiably, constantly stare,
You're jealous, often touch, kiss everywhere,
Like a lover. I say "I'm ready," but you stall:
You're nothing like a lover then at all.

XI

In dead of night, drenched by thick-falling rain,
Did I deceive my husband, come to you
To sit here doing nothing, and refrain
From making love, as lovers ought to do?

XII

Oh lovely lady, wait for me!
   What is your pretty name?
Where do you live? Whatever fee
   You ask, you'll find I'm game.

Won't talk? Where is your place? I'll send
   Someone with you that way.
You've someone else? My haughty friend,
   Good-bye! Won't "good-bye" say?

I'll seek you out one time, then two,
   And yet again, for I
Can soften tougher ones than you.
   But girl, for now, good-bye!

XIII

Hello there. "And hello to you." Your name?
"And yours?" Slow down, not yet. "You do the same."
You have someone? "Love takes no holiday."
Well, do you want to dine with me today?
"If you would like." Sure, how much will it be?
"Don't pay me first." That's strange. "But you should see
How much in bed I'm worth, then pay." You're fair.
Where do you live? I'll send my servant there.
"Just ask around." When will you come? "You say
What time you wish." Right now! "Then lead the way."

XIV

Xanthíppe's conversation and her singing,
    Her harp and her expressive eyes,
    The flame beginning to arise
In her just now, oh heart, to you are bringing
A blaze, I don't know how or why or when.
You'll start to smolder, poor thing. You'll know then.

XV

I fell in love. Who hasn't? Then I went
    On revels, but who hasn't spent
Time reveling? If crazy I became,
    Who but a god can be to blame?
Let this be cast aside. Where black had been,
    Already gray hair rushes in,
To me "it is the age of wisdom" saying.
    I played when it was time for playing;
But since that time is gone and won't return,
    I'll find some loftier concern.

XVI

With thirty-seven transits of the sun,
Like pages torn from life, already done,
Already on my hair the flecks of gray,
Xanthíppe, "it's the age of wisdom" say,
But still for harps and revels I've a yearning,
And fire in my insatiate heart is burning.
Quick, Muses, write "Xanthíppe," she can be
The flourish that ends my insanity.

XVII

White violets again to intertwine,
  Again harp playing, Chian wine,
And Syrian myrrh to have again, once more
  To revel, have a drunken whore,
I do not want. Such madness I can't bear.
  But with narcissus bind my hair,
Give me a taste of flute, let my lungs ooze
  With Mitylenaían wine, suffuse
My limbs with saffron oil, and have me wed
  A girl who's kept to her own bed.

XVIII

Let, Philainís, the lamp fresh oil imbibe,
Mute witness of what words should not describe,
Then leave. For Love alone dislikes the sight
Of animate observers. Pull the door tight.
And you, Xanthó, love-loving wife, now see
What Aphrodite's left to you and me.

XIX

Tomorrow, Piso, your Muse-loving friend
Drags you to his spare cottage, to attend
The feast of Epicurus, and to dine
With us at three o'clock. No Chian wine,
And no sow udder will you have; instead,
You'll see your truest friends, and you'll be read
Much sweeter words than the Phæacians knew.
And if, to even us, at some time you
Would turn an eye, then Piso, we will share
A fatter feast in place of my plain fare.

XX

Before five times and even nine,
  Now, Aphrodite, one
I scarcely do from day's decline
  Till coming of the sun;

And even my thing, woe is me!
  Will often start half-dead,
And then die imperceptibly,
  That wretched hammerhead!

Ah Old Age, Old Age, if some day
  You come to me, I who
Already like this waste away,
  What are you going to do?

EXPLANATORY NOTES

I (GP 41 Meleager, AP 5.24)

Philodemos must have read many love epigrams before he began writing his own poetry, since so many of his poems pick up the motifs and themes of his predecessors. This epigram reminds us of the "half of my soul's still living" of Callimachus XXII, but even more of the dialogue between reason and passion in Meleager V. Meleager says his heart cannot be expected to follow the dictates of his rational soul, since love took away the will even from Zeus. In a similar vein, the narrator in this poem—even when warned—is powerless to avoid falling in love. Philodemos may be signaling the relationship of his poem to Meleager's verse by using Heliodora as the name of the woman (see Meleager XXIII–XXV).

II (GP 16, AP 12.173)

The name Thermion means "little hot one." "Demo" may have been borrowed from Meleager (see his poem XVI), but the theme of Philodemos's epigram owes more to Callimachus XX:

> Whatever flees I know how to pursue,
> But something that's already come to lie
> In easy reach, I quickly pass on by.

The comparison between the easy and hard-to-get woman appears also in Philodemos V, which takes just the opposite point of view. It turns up later in several Latin poems: for example, in Horace *Satires* 1.2 (see notes to epigrams IV and V below) and in Martial 1.57, which counsels a middle way:

> You ask me, Flaccus, what girl I should woo?
> One not too easy or too hard to do.
> I like the kind that's halfway in between,
> Not too much trouble, but not too routine.

III (GP 6, AP 5.115)

Paphos was the mythical birthplace of Aphrodite, so it is little wonder that the poet fell in love with the first Demo. The same goes for the second, who was from Samos, which had a reputation for attractive courtesans. The identification of the third city is disputed; I have followed Gow and Page and given it as Nysa, but the exact name isn't important—provided it is of a city a bit off the beaten track. Argos is in the eastern Peloponnese south of Corinth. History does not record the particular attractions of girls from Nysa and Argos, but that is just the point. The poet says he fell in love with the first two Demos from regions of Greece known for gorgeous women, and that this was no surprise. But the third Demo was no longer a joke because she *didn't* come from Paphos or Samos but came from Nysa (where's that?). It is as if the poet had used New York and Los Angeles for the first two girls, then Allentown and Oklahoma City. One model for this poem may have been an epigram of Meleager (GP 98, *AP* 12.165), in which the poet gives his name as explanation of his love of boys of different colors, since the name "Meleager" seems to join black (*melas*) with white (*argos*). Needless to say, this etymology is just as unlikely as the one Philodemos gives. David Sider (in *Epigrams of Philodemos*) points out that another model may have been a second epigram of Meleager (GP 26, *AP* 5.160), also about a Demo:

> Someone stays warm as he above you lies,
> Demó of fair cheeks, and my heart now sighs.
> No big surprise if it's a Jew you've got:
> Even on cold Sabbaths, Eros is hot.

This poem makes similar use of *mega thauma,* "big surprise," and mentions love that is *thermos,* "hot." Sabbaths may have been cold for the Jews because on that day they were prohibited from gathering firewood and lighting fires.

IV (GP 3, AP 5.25)

Kydilla cannot be a prostitute, or there would be no danger to the narrator. The poem makes sense only if she is someone else's wife and the narrator is risking the punishment of an adulterer, which according to Horace (*Satires* 1.2.37–46) could include a hefty fine, castration, death by flogging, or drenching with the urine of servant boys.

V (GP 25, AP 5.126)

Another epigram about an adulterer who wouldn't be shivering with fear unless he were afraid of being caught. Even his name and his lover's are hush-hush. In IV we sympathize with the narrator, who knows he risks his life (or worse) every time he makes love but who cannot help himself.

In V, the same behavior becomes the butt of the poet's joke. The sentiment is the opposite of that in II: now Philodemos says we shouldn't bother with women who are "under lock and key," it isn't worth the trouble. In *Satires* 1.2.120–22, Horace mentions Philodemos by name and cites him for saying that the best women don't cost much and come when called. He may be referring to this poem, but it is also possible that Philodemos wrote several epigrams on this topic and that the allusion is to a poem that has not survived. In mythology, Lysianassa was one of the fifty nereids or sea nymphs. As Simone Beta has pointed out, the number twelve may have a special resonance, perhaps referring to twelve sexual positions. Aristophanes in *The Frogs* refers to a woman called Cyrene, a famous courtesan with the nickname "Twelve-tricks," and the Hellenistic Greek writer Paxamos wrote a book on making love called "Twelve Ways of Doing It," which unfortunately has not survived.

VI (GP 9, AP 5.123)

This epigram is unusual among the surviving epigrams of Philodemos. Gow and Page say that its "sensuous tone and exquisite phrasing" are "hardly to be found in any Greek author earlier than Meleager and Philodemos," and Sider (in *Epigrams of Philodemos*) calls it "in tone the most lyrical of Philodemos's epigrams." In mythology, Endymion was a Greek shepherd or hunter, in some accounts the son of Aethlios and grandson of Zeus. The goddess of the moon fell in love with him while he was sleeping, and Zeus put him to sleep forever, either as punishment or at his own or the goddess's request.

VII (GP 10, AP 5.124)

The next three poems I have selected were written in praise of women not conventionally attractive, this first of a girl too young for love. For the name Lysidike, see Asclepiades IV. The calyx is a leaflike layer of plant tissue that encloses a bud. In line 2 Philodemos uses the Greek word *botrys,* or "cluster of grapes," which here must refer to the girl's pudenda. Her "early maiden graces" would then be her pubic hair. The rest of the poem is, as Gow and Page say, "neatly expressed but conventional." This poem was the inspiration for *Odes* 2.5, one of Horace's finest poems, also about a young girl not yet ready for love, which borrows from Philodemos both the unripe fruit and the grapes still not dark:

Not yet the yoke can she with bowed neck pull,
Not yet connubial duties tolerate,
　　Nor of the brute stampeding bull
　　Endure in love the heavy weight.

The heart of your young heifer still is there
Among the fields, seeking on summer days
　　Relief in streams from heavy air,
　　Or eager in moist willow plays

With the young calves. Cupidity, then, stay
For this still unripe fruit; Fall will imbue
　　With changing colors grapes from gray
　　Soon to a seasoned purple hue.

Soon she will follow: Fierce time will endow
Her with those years that they will confiscate
　　From you, and soon with shameless brow
　　Lalágë will seek out her mate;

More loved then than Pholóë, prone to flee;
Or Chlóris, whose pale shoulders shine with light
　　Like moon glow glancing from the sea,
　　Resplendent through the limpid night;

Or Gýges, who if put among the girls
Still to discerning guests would seem in place,
　　Distinction lost in loosened curls
　　And an indeterminate face.

VIII (GP 2, AP 5.13)

This second poem provides a counterbalance to the first: now the woman
is too old normally to be considered attractive but has fortunately man-
aged to avoid the gray hair, drooping breasts, and wrinkled skin expected
of a woman her age. There is a lovely contrast between the dark color of
her long trailing hair and the paleness of her marble breasts. The name
Charito is derived from the Greek word *charis,* meaning "charm," a
word that reappears later in the poem in the phrase "charms of every
kind."

IX (GP 8, AP 5.121)

In the last of these three poems, the poet says that Philainion is not con-
ventionally attractive because she is small and dark, which were less
desirable features to the Greeks and Romans. She nevertheless has other
compensating qualities, including her accommodating nature. Aphro-
dite's girdle is described in *Iliad* 14.214–17:

> So Aphrodite said, and then removed
> The girdle from her breast, embroidered cloth
> Of ornate art in which her magic lay:
> The love and yearning and sweet winning words
> That rob the reason even of the wise.

X and XI (GP 13, AP 5.306 and GP 7, AP 5.120)

Two epigrams, both of four lines with a similar theme of a woman com-
plaining about the reluctance of her lover to go to bed. It is rare in Greek
love epigram for the voice of the poem to be a woman's; I have given only
two previous examples, Asclepiades XV in which a woman laments the
loss of love, and Meleager XXIX (also attributed to Philodemos) in
which a woman complains of her lover's infidelity. Both of these poems
have an innocence about them suggestive of young love. There is no

mention of sex and no reason to suppose that the woman is an adulteress. In Philodemos X and XI, on the other hand, sex is the whole point of contention. The woman in XI provides an amusing contrast to the man in IV. Both poems are about adultery, but the man in IV is obsessed by the risk he is taking, whereas the woman in XI seems much nobler and braver. "Come on," she says in effect, "get over it, let's have some fun!" The dead of night and drenching rain are conventional; see, for example, Asclepiades XI and XII.

XII and XIII (GP 14 Antiphilus, AP 5.308 and GP 4, AP 5.46)

These two poems consist entirely of monologue or dialogue, as do Callimachus VI–VII and Meleager V, XXVI, and XXVII. The conversation is colloquial and takes place on the street, much as in a Greek mime (see notes to Meleager XXVI and XXVII). The first epigram is a monologue ceaselessly striving to become a dialogue, but the man's attempts to get the woman to speak meet with no success. We are given no description of the woman other than that she is *kompse*—"lovely," as I have translated, but the word can also mean "elegant" or "well-dressed." Gigante says that "it is certain only that the woman is not a prostitute," but in fact nothing is certain at all. This ambiguity provides much of the charm and interest of the poem. In the second epigram, the woman is clearly a streetwalker, and a saucy one at that. Her "attitude" however seems part of her act, promising from her forwardness a similar lack of restraint in bed. The ending of XIII is exactly the opposite of XII: instead of refusal the man gets everything he wants, and the last word of the poem is *proage,* "lead the way."

XIV (GP 11, AP 5.131)

The poet describes the beginning of his relationship with Xanthippe, a woman he says becomes his wife (see the introduction to this chapter and XVIII). It is surprisingly conventional for a work written by a man about the woman who he says was the love of his life, but it has one unusual feature: it is rare for a male poet to mention the passion of the woman. Asclepiades in XVII describes the cheeks of Didyme, which glow red with emotion, but Didyme's love is more likely to have been for Ptolemy Philadelphus than for the poet. In Philodemos's poem, in contrast, the woman's love for the poet is an important part of her attractiveness to him. There is of course nothing new in this: many a man falls for a woman after she lets him see her feeling. It is nevertheless an indication that Philodemos may have seen his relationship with Xanthippe as something different from the one he had (or says he had) with the other women in his poems.

XV (GP 18, AP 5.112)

The first of three I have translated in which Philodemos renounces reveling in favor of philosophy and marriage. More than a hundred years ago, the German scholar Georg Kaibel pointed out that this poem of Philodemos was written in response to Meleager V. Meleager casts reason aside to pursue reveling and love, but Philodemos in his poem says he is doing just the opposite. Philodemos makes the relationship to Meleager's poem explicit by using a rare form (a third-person singular, passive perfect imperative) of the same verb as in Meleager, *rhipto,* meaning to "throw," or "cast aside." He places the verb at the beginning of a line, as Meleager also does, and in a similar construction. But in Meleager reason is cast aside for reveling, whereas in Philodemos it is just the other way around.

XVI (GP 17, AP 11.41)

This poem is clearly related to the previous epigram, since both say that gray hair announces the "age of wisdom," using exactly the same words (though with one change from singular to plural) and in the same position in the fourth line of both poems. What makes this second epigram different, however, is the explicit mention of Xanthippe, the woman Philodemos later calls his wife. The poet begins by saying that thirty-seven years have been torn from the book of his life. We are, I think, meant to imagine not just any book but a metaphorical book of love poetry from which the columns of writing or leaves have been torn. The number thirty-seven is significant, since, as Sider has pointed out in *Epigrams of Philodemos,* this is the age Aristotle says a man should marry. The poet is saying that even though he has come to the "age of wisdom," when it is time to turn to philosophy, he still finds himself unable to quell his lust. The solution he proposes is to have the Muses write Xanthippe in his metaphorical book of love poems as a flourish ending the madness of his debauchery. The word here for "flourish" is *koronis,* a special mark the Greeks put at the end of a section of a poetry book or the entire book. Meleager refers explicitly to the *koronis* in a poem I haven't translated (GP 129, *AP* 12.257), which was the last poem in his *Garland.* Philodemos is saying that Xanthippe will mark the end of the poet's reveling and of a certain sort of love poetry, since she will become his last lover, his wife.

XVII (GP 21, AP 11.34)

This is one of the cleverest of Philodemos's epigrams. The opening list of white violets, harp playing, Chian wine, and Syrian myrrh seems to be introducing yet another poem about a drinking party, but this expectation is disappointed at the beginning of the fourth line (the fifth in my translation) with *ouk ethelo,* "I do not want." Such a list at the beginning of a poem is called a priamel, and it usually consists of what the poet isn't going to say or doesn't like, thereby serving as a foil for his own choice or preference. This method of organizing the matter of a poem is as old as Sappho and Pindar, and we saw earlier examples in Asclepiades V and Callimachus XXI. What follows in Philodemos's poem is another list of a different flower and musical instrument, a different kind of wine, and saffron oil instead of myrrh. Although scholars once thought the slight differences in the two lists were significant, there is now nearly universal agreement that the whole point of the poem is that there is no difference— except, that is, for the woman. Instead of a drunken whore, Philodemos now wants to get married, and not to a courtesan but to a stay-at-home virgin. This becomes clear only in the last line of the poem. Sider has suggested (in "The Love Poetry of Philodemus") that this epigram may have served as a wedding invitation with the promise of a good party. If so, another poem (*AP* 5.80), once falsely attributed to Plato and now thought to have been written by Philodemos, may have served as his engagement proposal:

> I am an apple that a lover sent.
> Say "yes," Xanthippe. Soon our youth is spent.

XVIII (GP 1, AP 5.4)

A poem with a clever beginning. We expect Philainis to be yet another of the poet's lovers, and the mention of an oil lamp reinforces this feeling, since lamps are so often a part of Hellenistic love poetry (see, for example, Asclepiades XX; Meleager XXIX, XXX). But our expectation is abruptly confounded at the beginning of the third line by the word *exithi,* "leave." The poet then turns to Xanthippe, "Xantho" for short, who is now his wife. We are perhaps meant to imagine the couple on their wedding night, with the husband more experienced than his young spouse (though see epigram XIV).

XIX (GP 23, AP 11.44)

One of the very first examples of an "invitation poem," a genre of which we have examples also of Philodemos's contemporary Catullus, then later of Horace and Martial, and much later still of Ben Jonson in "Inviting a Friend to Supper." It is one of only a few of Philodemos's epigrams that we know to have been written in Italy. The Piso of the poem is L. Calpurnius Piso Caesoninus, Philodemos's friend and probably patron (see the introduction to this chapter). The "feast of Epicurus" is identified in the Greek simply as the "Twentieth," since it was held on the twentieth of the month. Three o'clock was a common time for dinner. Chian wine came from the island of Chios, located in the eastern Aegean off the coast of present-day Turkey. This wine was famous in antiquity and very expensive, the Greek and Roman equivalent of a *premier cru* such as Château Margaux or Château Latour. Sow udder was also a delicacy. That expensive wine and sow udder were *not* going to be served may have been intended to indicate the poet's financial condition; it was probably also meant to signal the Epicurean nature of the feast, since Epicurus advised his followers to be content with little. The Phæacians lived in a mythical island to which Ulysses was swept after leaving Calypso. Epicurus was sometimes falsely accused of taking his doctrine of pleasure from Homer's famous description of the merriment at the feast of the Phæacians at the beginning of book 9 of the *Odyssey*. The "words . . . the Phæacians knew" were the verses recited by Ulysses to King Alcinous and his court, which constitute books IX–XII of the *Odyssey*. They tell the tale of the wandering of Ulysses after leaving Troy and include the most famous adventures in the epic, such as his encounters with the Lotus Eaters, the Cyclops Polyphemus, Circe, and the sirens; his visit to the underworld; and the passage through Scylla and Charybdis. The "sweeter words" promised to Piso may have been those of Epicurean philosophers. The ending of the poem has been variously interpreted. Some scholars believe that Philodemos is merely saying that if Piso were to come to his feast, the feast would be richer for his presence. I agree, however, with Gow and Page and with Sider (in *Epigrams of Philodemos*), believing that a more natural reading of the Greek is that Philodemos is asking for Piso to become a more regular participant in the gatherings of Epicureans and to become the poet's patron, as he seems eventually to have done.

XX (GP 27, AP 11.30)

This poem has been the subject of much scholarly discussion, summarized at length by Gigante and Sider. I mostly agree with Sider's interpretation, with one exception. Philodemos says that his thing will die *kata brachu,* which normally means "little by little" and which I have translated as "imperceptibly." Sider thinks instead that *kata brachu* means "briefly, for a short time," citing a passage from Philodemos's prose works where the phrase may in fact have that meaning (see *Epigrams of Philodemos*). Philodemos could then be saying that he has trouble getting it up, and even when he does, it doesn't stay up for long. Our interpretations may not be terribly different, provided we agree that Philodemos is *not* complaining of premature ejaculation, which is rare among the elderly. R. F. Thomas accepts the translation "little by little" but thinks Philodemos is saying "that the act from start to finish now takes all night." This seems to me physiologically improbable. Besides, if the poet could last all night in a single go, why would he be complaining? The poet calls his member "that wretched hammerhead." In Greek this is *touto to Termerion,* "that Termerian thing," after Termeros, a mythical highwayman who killed people by butting them with his head.

CHAPTER TEN

Lucillius

If an epigram in English is a short, amusing poem with a clever ending, then the credit (and blame) goes first to Lucillius. Like Leonidas, Callimachus, and the other poets of Meleager's *Garland,* Lucillius grounded his poems in the form of actual inscriptions—epitaphs and dedications, as well as monument inscriptions on the bases of statues of famous athletes. He differed from his predecessors, however, in that he used this tradition to write poems that were almost entirely satirical in nature, poking fun at generic types rather than actual historical figures. Poems like this had been written before; Leonidas VI is an excellent example.

What distinguishes Lucillius from his predecessors is his almost exclusive devotion to this sort of poem. We have no record of how his epigrams were received among his contemporaries, but a very large number survived, almost as many as we have from Meleager and about the same number as from Callimachus, Asclepiades, and Philodemos combined. Lucillius and his younger disciple Nicarchus had a huge influence on the poetry of Martial and nearly all later poets of epigrams, both Greek and Latin, an influence that proved decisive for the future of the genre.

Lucillius is not mentioned in any of the writings of other Greek or Roman authors. Apart from a few tentative inferences we can draw from the poetry itself, we know nothing about who he was or where he came from. He appears to have written most of his poetry during the reign of the emperor Nero, whom he addresses in several of his poems. Like Philodemos before him, Lucillius was probably a Greek intellectual trying to make his way in Roman society; but during the hundred years separating Philodemos and Lucillius, Rome had changed almost beyond recognition. The moral and political issues of the day were no longer openly debated, and supreme power was held by the emperor, who could command the death of anyone who displeased him. The safest way for Lucillius to achieve prominence and still survive in this climate was to attach himself to Nero's court, and this seems to be what he did. In one of his epigrams (*AP* 9.572), Lucillius is pondering what sort of proem or introductory preface he should write for his second book of poetry. The epigram concludes:

> So now some prelude I too must provide
> To start my second book. What would be proper?
> "Olympian Muses, daughters of Zeus, I'd have died,
> If Nero hadn't given me some copper."

This seems to indicate that Nero was in some sense the poet's patron, although the word Lucillius uses for money, *chalkos* (copper), was the metal from which the cheapest coins were made. Some scholars have suggested that the amount of money Lucillius received must have been small, and that the poem may even have been implicitly critical of the emperor, but it is also possible that this was a joke of some sort between the poet and his ruler.

Nero was a fanatical enthusiast of Greek poetry and song. He learned to play the lyre and sang Greek lyric poetry in contests, first in Naples and then in Greece itself. The historian Cassius Dio in the second or third century CE wrote that "according to report," the emperor had a "slight and indistinct voice." Tacitus in his *Annals* claims that Nero pretended to show great anxiety about the outcome of the competitions but always won first prize and was enthusiastically applauded by supporters he is said to have paid. Suetonius in his *Lives of the Caesars* says that while Nero was singing, no one was allowed to leave the performance, and that women were reported to have given birth inside the theater. The Roman senator and Stoic philosopher P. Clodius Thrasea Paetus is said to have been executed in part because he refused to listen to the emperor sing.

Tacitus (*Annals* 14.16) describes poets gathering around Nero, who "sat with one another stringing together verses either brought from home or invented on the spot, and they filled in the emperor's words in whatever manner he had tossed them out. We can see this from the sort of poems these were, not flowing with any inspiration or vigor or unity." There can be little doubt that Tacitus, in his customary dour and disapproving manner, is describing poets who wrote epigrams, and that Lucillius was likely to have been among their number. It is easy for us now to understand and sympathize with Tacitus's enmity toward anyone who associated with an emperor who killed so many prominent citizens, but what was Lucillius supposed to do? He wrote amusing poems the emperor must clearly have enjoyed, and if the poems seem now to us a bit frivolous and decadent, so was Nero, and in spades!

A satirical poet who wrote for the court of Nero had to choose his targets with great care. It would have been dangerous to write poems making fun of actual people, especially for a Greek in Rome whose life was so easily expendable. This probably explains the generic nature of Lucillius's poems. Although the great majority contain names both Greek and Latin that purportedly belong to specific individuals, there is every likelihood that these names were made up. Patronymics are rarely given, and the same name could be used in different poems: for example, "Markos" of a runner in one poem (VII), a poet in another (XVI), and a hunter in a third (XXI). In some poems the names are clearly fabricated, such as "Olympikos" for a boxer (III) and "Makron" (Large) for a man no bigger than a mouse (XXIX).

The subjects of the poems are also generic. Lucillius took as the target of his wit other poets, grammarians, lawyers, orators, philosophers (especially Cynic philosophers), astrologers, singers, actors, painters, ship captains, farmers, dancers, doctors, misers, thieves, homosexuals, cuckolds, and women, as well as people who were covetous, lazy, or cowardly, or were too short, too tall, too thin, or too light. He made fun of hosts who read too much of their poetry during dinner or spent more money on silver plate than on food, and of guests who hoarded dishes during the banquet to take home afterward. A great many of these topics were later taken up by Martial, as I show in the notes with particular examples.

Among the most interesting and amusing of Lucillius's epigrams are those on Greek athletes. The Greeks held four series of panhellenic games: the Pythian Games at Delphi, in honor of Apollo; the Olympic Games, in honor of Zeus at Olympia in the northwest of the Peloponnese; the Nemean Games, also in honor of Zeus, near Nemea in the northeast of the Peloponnese; and the Isthmian Games at Corinth, in honor of Poseidon, god of the sea. Then, as now, great honor and esteem were awarded to a victor in the games—indeed, not only to the athlete but to his family (especially his father) and his hometown. Statues of the victors were often erected, and though few of these survive, we have many remaining examples of bases on which the statues had been placed.

These bases often have inscriptions. Here is one, appearing on a yellow-marble pedestal of a bronze statue (now lost), thought to date from around the beginning of the fourth century BCE (Ebert 32):

I'm Xenoklés, Euthýphron's son,
I wrestled four boys one by one;
   Without a fall,
   I took them all.

The voice of the poem is the athlete himself, who won each of his bouts
without falling once, a point of pride for wrestlers that is mentioned in
several inscriptions. Another poem, also dating from the fourth century
BCE, sat below a statue that probably represented a chariot, though the
statue has again been lost. This monument celebrated the chariot victo-
ries at the Isthmian and Pythian Games of Archon, a Macedonian from
Pella, who was an officer of Alexander the Great and was later appointed
satrap of Babylon. This time, rather than speaking himself, the victor is
directly addressed in the second person (Ebert 46):

Blest Árchon, twice with steeds you got the crown
At Isthmia and Delphi. Great renown
Comcs to your father from his son's good name,
And your home Pella has eternal fame.

Lucillius adopted the conventions of these inscriptions in trenchant
parodies, which came to the attention of scholars through an influential
article by the French philologist Louis Robert. Robert showed in great
detail how Lucillius carefully adopted the forms and technical terms of
athletic inscriptions. Robert's scholarship demonstrated that the epigrams
of Lucillius are more complex than they seem at first glance, and he
brought to them a much deeper appreciation than they had hitherto been
given. Though Robert's admiration for Lucillius has not always been sec-
onded, everyone would agree that Lucillius is often quietly amusing, occa-
sionally uproariously funny, and one of the most important of the Greek
poets of epigrams. He is therefore aptly placed at the end of this book. It
was Lucillius who determined many of the themes and even some aspects
of the style of the poetry of Martial, who arrived in Rome in 64 CE, just
four years before Nero's death. Martial also wrote satirical poems of a

generic nature, and even more deliberately than Lucillius he attempted to construct his poems with great care in order to produce a clever ending. Since the European poets of the Renaissance could as a rule read Latin but not Greek, it was Martial (through Lucillius), rather than Callimachus or Meleager, who shaped the form of the genre we still have today.

I

To Zeus, the boxer Aúlos dedicated
His skull from bones he, one by one, located;
If Nemea doesn't kill him, maybe he'll
Give too the vertebrae he has left still.

II

At all the contests where the Greeks appear,
I boxed, Andróleos, at every one.
My prize at Pisa was to save one ear,
At Plátaia, one eyelid's what I won.

At Delphi I was carried out as dead;
My father and the townsfolk were proclaimed,
And told to lift me up so I'd be led
Out of the stadium, a corpse or maimed.

III

This man Olympikós whom now you see,
   Augustus, had a nose,
Chin, forehead, ears and eyelids, and then he
   A boxer's calling chose,

And lost them all, so that his birthright too
   He couldn't even claim;
His brother put his portrait up to view:
   The court said, "Not the same!"

IV

Your head, Apollophánes, has the look
Of a sieve or the edge of a worm-eaten book,
With holes like those that ants or thongs create,
Like Lydian notes for lyres, crooked and straight.
Still fearless, box! If you're hit as before,
You'll have the scars you have. You can't have more.

V

Kleómbrotos, a boxer who retired,
Got married, and in his house then acquired
An Isthmia and Nemea of blows,
A fighting hag worse than his former foes,
Who lands Olympic punches, and can bring
More fear to him at home than in the ring.
When he revives, he's flayed to give his due,
And even if he gives it, he's flayed too.

VI

No wrestler was more rapidly
Among contestants on his back,
No runner ever could like me
So slowly run around the track;

In discus not at all could I
Come close enough so I'd compete;
I never once could qualify
In jumping, couldn't lift my feet;

A cripple would much further drive
The javelin. I was the first
Who, in pentathlon, was all five
Times heralded to be the worst.

VII

Once Markos ran in armor till midnight,
So that the stadium was locked up tight.
You see, the guards all thought him to be one
Of the stone soldiers, there for some deed he'd done.
What then? Next year, they opened up the place,
There's Markos, still about to start the race.

VIII

To sacred games the wrestler Milon went,
And was the only one in his event.
At once the judge called his name for the crown,
But he walked out and on his hip slid down.
"Don't wreath that man," the crowd began to call,
"Since he was by himself and took a fall!"
The wrestler stood and "Not three times!" cried out;
"Let someone throw me in another bout!"

IX

You dance according to the book
    In every way, but one
Important thing you overlook,
    We're sad it wasn't done.

You danced Niobe, there you stood
    Like stone, you did that well;
As Kapaneús, too, you were good,
    Out of the blue you fell;

But then you danced Kanákë all
    Amiss: you weren't yet dead,
But took your sword and left the hall.
    That's not the tale we read!

X

The sea we sail, oh Dionysius, true!
   This ship's got water everywhere,
   The Adriatic's nearly bare,
It's in our boat, and the Aegean too!

Put on your arms, oh Caesar! Soon we'll be
   No craft but Ocean's wooden stream,
   And Dionysius starts to seem
Not captain of a ship but of the sea!

XI

Menískos took from Zeus's garden three
Gold fruit, like Hercules before. When he
Was caught, to all a great sight he became,
Like Hercules, alive and set aflame.

XII

I never, Epikrátes, knew
That you could play the flute or sing
Or act, or any other thing
That needs a chorus next to you.

Though I invited you alone,
You came from home with dancers here,
And all the food back to the rear
You pass to them. Since you have shown

The way that we are going to eat,
Go tell your slaves that they recline,
So in our places they can dine,
And let us go stand at their feet.

XIII

Someone to silver famine summons me,
Spreads out his hungry plates for all to see,
But vexed by shining silver I declare,
"Where is the feasting of my earthenware?"

XIV

You give me raw beef as hors d'œuvre,
  A slice or so, then fill
Three glasses from the mix you serve
  Of wine that's rawer still.

At once with epigrams then you
  Deluge me; were I one
Of those friends of Ulysses, who
  Ate cattle of the Sun,

Then impious like them, oh may
  I gulp the ocean's swell;
But if the sea's too far away,
  Then throw me in a well!

XV

A poet's truly excellent, who feeds
His dinner guests once his poems have been read.
But may his zeal recoil on him, who reads
And sends his guests back home again unfed.

XVI

This tomb, oh passerby, though no one died,
The poet Markos built, and then supplied
The epigram that on this stone appears:
"Come weep for Máximos, who lived twelve years."
I've not seen any Máximos, but say
To you to read this, and weep anyway.

XVII

I hate, Lord Caesar, those whom no young man
Could satisfy, not even if he can
Write "Sing, oh Goddess, wrath"; but that unless,
Half-bald, as old as Priam, he'd possess
A back bent over, he would never please,
Could never even write his ABC's.
If this is how the land, oh High Zeus, lies,
Then only those with hernias are wise.

XVIII

Onésimos the boxer came to see
The prophet Ólympos, to learn if he
Would live long. "If," the sage said, "you resign,
But if you box, then Saturn is your sign."

XIX

Astrologers with one voice prophesied
Long years would pass before my uncle died.
Just Hermokleídes rapid death foretold,
But said this with the corpse already cold.

XX

When Aúlos fixed his own birth chart, he said
His fated hour had come, and he'd be dead
In four hours. But still living after five,
And fated to know nothing and survive,
Ashamed, he hanged himself. Up high suspended,
He dies, and knowing nothing has life ended.

XXI

To Pan of grottos, nymphs who roam the hill,
And to the satyrs, Markos, who could kill
Not one thing with his dogs and his boar-spear,
In place of game the dogs themselves hung here.

XXII

A small farm Menophánes bought, then he
From hunger hanged himself from a neighbor's tree.
His farm had soil too sparse to make the tomb,
So for a price next door they found the room.
Had Epicurus known, he'd have proposed
Of farms, not atoms, all things were composed.

XXIII

Oh bloody Ares, man's bane, Barber, stop!
There's nothing left of me still you can chop;
   Cut lower! Pass to muscles now
   Beneath my knees, that I allow.
This place is full of flies. More of your blows,
And you'll see vultures, flocks of carrion crows.

XXIV

I lost an ox, one nanny goat, a pig,
Because of them you've, Meneklés, your fee.
For Othryádas I don't give a fig,
Nor are the thieves men from Thermopylae.

I'm suing Eutychídes, so then why
Would Xerxes and the Spartans bring me glory?
Unless you mention me, out loud I'll cry:
"The pig, not Meneklés, should tell this story!"

XXV

She says he teaches grammar to her boy,
That bearded Ménandros in her employ.
But he shows her at night without cessation
Conjunctions, endings, forms of conjugation.

XXVI

Once Diophón with envy nearly died,
    Seeing nearby
    Another, up high
On a taller cross than his own, crucified.

XXVII

Stingy Asclepiádes saw a mouse,
"What are you doing," said he, "in my house?"
The mouse laughed sweetly; "Don't fear, friend," he said,
"I don't seek food in your place, just a bed."

XXVIII

    Chairémon, lighter than
    A piece of chaff or bran,
Flew up, raised by a light breeze one fair day,
And probably would have been swept away,

    But with his feet he clung
    To a spider's web, and hung
There on his back five days and nights, then fled
By climbing on the sixth day down a thread.

XXIX

A mouse found Makron dozing in the heat,
And dragged him to a mouse hole by his feet.
Unarmed, he gave the mouse's throat a squeeze,
And said, "Look Zeus! A second Hercules!"

XXX

Oh Erasístratos, your horse may be
   Thessalian, but you can't make
   Him totter to and fro, or shake
His limbs with drugs from all of Thessaly.

So wooden is your horse, if you'd employ
   All Trojan and Greek soldiers too,
   You'd not together drag him through
The Scæan Gate to enter into Troy.

If you'd take my advice, here's what I think:
   Make him a statue, dedicate
   Him to some god, decorticate
His feed and make a children's barley drink.

EXPLANATORY NOTES

I (AP 11.258)

The first eight poems I have selected are all parodies of monument epigrams placed below statues of athletes, like those I described in the introduction to the chapter. Although the poems are intended to be satirical, many nevertheless retain conventions of actual inscriptions. This first poem begins like a dedication, as do, for example, Leonidas XV–XVIII and Callimachus XIII–XVIII. The boxer, however, is dedicating his own skull. As Louis Robert pointed out, the word for skull in Greek is very similar to the word for helmet, an object often dedicated by warriors and found in many ancient tombs. The word for "vertebrae" can also mean "knucklebones," and these too were often dedicated and found in tombs, especially of children. This poem is typical of Lucillius, gruesome but with a wry sense of humor and acute appreciation of the absurd.

II (AP 11.81)

Like many existing inscriptions, this epigram begins as if in vainglorious pronouncement of triumph: "At all the contests where the Greeks appear." We next expect to hear of the boxer's many victories, but instead the epigram says merely that Androleos showed up everywhere as a participant. Pisa, a town near Olympia, is used here to indicate the Olympic Games. Plataia (also spelled Platæa) was a city in southern Boeotia, south of Thebes and northwest of Athens, where the army of Xerxes was decisively defeated and driven from Greece in 479 BCE. Games in celebration of that victory were held in honor of Zeus Eleutherios (the Deliverer); though not originally among the principal panhellenic games, according to Robert they assumed increasing importance and by the first century CE were greatly esteemed. Inscriptions often list the prizes won at various tournaments, and Lucillius parodies this fashion by using the same verb for "win" normally found in athletic inscriptions. What Androleos says he won, however, tells us instead what he lost. At the end of the epigram, the athlete's father and his townsfolk are "proclaimed," again as in many inscriptions. I noted in the introduction to this chapter how the father and city were thought to win renown from an athlete's victory. Here, however, the verb Lucillius uses has more the sense of "summoned." We can almost hear from the loudspeaker, "Will the parents of Androleos son of Damoteles please come and help him out of the stadium."

III (AP 11.75)

Another poem with a pompous beginning, parodying many an inscription placed on the base of a statue of a victorious athlete. Even the name of the athlete, "Olympikos," is chosen to give the impression of greatness. In the second line of my translation, the poet addresses "Augustus," an epithet commonly used to refer to any of the Roman emperors and not necessarily Octavian. Here it almost certainly is meant for Nero. As in both epigrams I and II, the poem satirizes the brutality of the ancient sport of boxing, in which injuries especially to the face were commonplace. Another epigram of Lucillius (*AP* 11.76) has a similar theme and also uses the name Olympikos, though that is of course no guarantee that the two poems are intended to be about the same boxer. They nevertheless come to pretty much the same conclusion:

> Olympikós, with that mug don't go near
> A well, don't look in any pool that's clear.
> If like Narcissus, you would catch your eye,
> You'd hate yourself to death, and then you'd die.

IV (AP 11.78)

This poem, though again about injuries to the head in boxing, differs in tone from the previous three, since there is no triumphant beginning and no attempt to give the impression of an actual monument epigram. The "holes like those that ants or thongs create" is my attempt to translate a pun. Lucillius says that the holes are of *myrmekes,* which normally means "ants" but which can also refer to boxing thongs. These were leather straps wrapped around the hands and wrists to protect the knuckles during the fight, but the thongs became gradually more damaging, containing stiff leather and even metal with terrible effect. Virgil in the *Aeneid* describes thongs that "were stiff with iron and lead sewn in" (5.405). The "Lydian notes" refer to the notes of the Lydian musical mode or scale. A Greek musical scale lacked a staff (that was the invention of Guido of Arezzo in the early eleventh century CE) but consisted instead of symbols derived from Greek capital letters that indicated different pitches. The notes, like the letters of the alphabet, were therefore "crooked and straight," just as Lucillius describes them.

V (AP 11.79)

This poem again plays on the conventions of athletic inscriptions. Here, the Isthmia and Nemea "acquired" by the boxer were not the prizes one normally expects to find in an inscription but rather "blows" like the ones delivered in those contests. While pillorying the boxer, the poem is also one of several of Lucillius's epigrams that make fun of women. Another of his epigrams (*AP* 11.310), for example, complains,

> You bought hair, rouge, wax, teeth; but in their place,
> For the same price, you could have bought a face.

And another (*AP* 11.240),

> Not just Demostratís smells of he-goat:
> She puts those breathing her breath in the same boat.

These poems are not Lucillius at his best but may have been favorably received by an emperor who killed his mother and his sick aunt, had one wife put to death, and is reported to have killed another wife by kicking her in the abdomen when she was pregnant. The poems Lucillius wrote making fun of women were the forerunners of the many poems by Martial on this same theme.

VI (AP 11.84)

There is an epigram in the *Anthologia Planudea* (*APl* 3), attributed to the sixth-century BCE poet Simonides but probably written much later by a Hellenistic imitator, that says:

> At Isthmia and Delphi, Diophón,
> Phílon's son,
> In jumping, discus, javelin, wrestling, and footrace
> Took first place.

Diophon was a contestant in the pentathlon, and these were the traditional five events. An athlete could win the pentathlon with victories in only three events; Diophon, winning all five, may have been an exceptional contestant. Since there is no mention of Diophon's hometown or patron deity, however, this poem is more likely to have been a literary exercise to see if the names of all five of the events could be accommodated in one verse. It is very likely to have been the inspiration for Lucillius's poem; we have the same five contests, but the athlete is defeated in all five instead of victorious.

VII (AP 11.85)

The *hoplitodromos,* or "race in armor," was a traditional Olympic event in which the runners ran a variable but usually short distance in full or partial armor. It was a test of strength and endurance as well as of speed. Robert gives several examples of actual inscriptions in which an athlete such as a boxer or wrestler was so strong that he continued fighting even through the night. Here we have an armed runner seemingly able also to run late into the night, and then to continue running for a whole year. We soon discover the true explanation: he never left the starting block.

VIII (AP 11.316)

The wrestler Milon (or Milo) of Croton was one of the most famous athletes of antiquity, winning so many times at Olympia that he must have been over forty at the time of his last competition. His strength was proverbial. He was said by Pausanias to have been able to break a cord tied around his head by holding his breath and swelling his veins. Another epigram, attributed to Simonides (*APl* 24), says that Milon during his wrestling victories "did not fall on his knees," resembling Xenokles of the inscription quoted in the introduction to this chapter who was "without a fall." Lucillius uses the name Milon for his wrestler, who came to compete at "sacred games." This phrase could describe any of the major athletic competitions in the Greek world, since they all occurred within a religious context and celebrated one of the gods. Milon discovered he was the only wrestler who had come in his event, presumably because he had scared off all the rest, and the rules specified that in that case he should be awarded the prize. Then Milon fell—not on his knees but even further down, onto his hip, and without an opponent. Nevertheless, as Milon exclaims in his defense, a wrestler had to be thrown three times to be defeated. Lucillius may have gotten the idea for this poem from an actual occurrence, but there is no evidence of such a thing happening to Milon of Croton.

IX (AP 11.254)

Niobe was a mortal woman who boasted that she was greater than Leto, because Leto had only two children (Apollo and Artemis), whereas she had (at least in some accounts) a total of fourteen—seven sons and seven daughters. Apollo then killed all of Niobe's sons, and Artemis all of her daughters, and Niobe in her grief turned into a stone fountain, endlessly bringing forth the water of her tears. Kapaneus was one of the "Seven against Thebes," described in the tragedy of that name by Aeschylus. As he was besieging Thebes, Kapaneus boasted that even Zeus could not stop him from entering the city, and Zeus punished Kapaneus by strik- ing him down with lightning as he was ascending a scaling ladder. In Greek mythology Kanake was a daughter of Aeolus, god of the winds. She fell in love with one of her brothers, and her father made her commit suicide. As Niobe, the dancer in the poem—a man, as the Greek makes clear—was stiff as a stone; and as Kapaneus, he fell down. So far, so good. But when he danced Kanake, he left the stage with his sword before he had killed himself. What is remarkable about this poem is that Suetonius tells us that Nero sang and acted the parts of both Niobe and Kanake, though Kapaneus isn't mentioned. Lucillius seems to come per- ilously close to criticizing Nero's dancing, even suggesting that the audi- ence was disappointed the emperor hadn't kill himself. Some scholars have claimed that Lucillius simply couldn't have gotten away with this, arguing that the poem must have been written before Nero danced these roles or after Nero died. Suetonius says that Nero was particularly lenient toward poets who made fun of him, but he and Cassius Dio also say that Nero was extraordinarily sensitive about his theatrical performances. It is difficult to believe that Lucillius read this poem to his ruler.

X (AP 11.247)

On first inspection, this poem appears to lampoon a ship so leaky that it more closely resembles the sea itself than a vessel sailing above the water. The name Lucillius uses for the captain of the ship, "Dionysius," is given in another of his poems for a shipbuilder (*AP* 11.246). In Homer the ocean was not a large body of water, as the word is presently used, but a continuous river or "stream" encircling the perimeter of the world. Although it is possible to read this poem as simple satire of a leaky ship, it may also have been written to make fun of Nero. The poem is addressed to "Caesar," a term that, like Augustus, could be used for any emperor and here again almost certainly was Nero (see also XVII). It was well-known in Rome that Nero had attempted to kill his mother by putting her on the Bay of Naples in a boat engineered to break up at sea. In the event, his mother managed to swim to shore but was later put to death by Nero's henchmen. It would be difficult for a contemporary not to think of this occurrence when reading the poem, especially since the poet addresses the emperor directly and tells him, "To arms!" According to Suetonius, the actor Datus was banished from Rome for singing a song that began, "Farewell to thee, father; farewell to thee, mother." As he sang the song, he made a pantomime of drinking (for Nero's father) and swimming (for Nero's mother). Nero's father by adoption, the emperor Claudius, was thought by many to have been killed by poisoning, though by Agrippina, Nero's mother, rather than by Nero himself. Again, it seems unlikely that Lucillius could have published this poem in Nero's lifetime.

XI (AP 11.184)

Perhaps the most difficult of the labors of Hercules was the gathering of the three golden fruit from the garden of the Hesperides on the northern edge of the world. These fruit, usually said to be apples (though the Greek has been variously interpreted), belonged to Zeus and Hera; they were difficult to find and carefully guarded. Like Hercules, Meniskos also took three fruit, but the Zeus from which he stole them was not the king of the gods but rather the emperor of Rome, who was often referred to as "Zeus on earth" and whom Lucillius also calls Zeus in epigram XVII. The fruit may not have been literally of gold but may have been called "golden" in the poem to signify that they were taken from the garden of the "Golden House." This huge, opulently decorated palace, "overlaid with gold and adorned with gems and mother-of-pearl" according to Suetonius, was built by Nero after his first palace had burned down. But Tacitus in his *Annals* says that even the jewels and gold were not as wonderful as the fields and lakes. Since the thief had taken the fruit from the emperor's garden, his crime was treason and worthy of a most horrible punishment. That brings us back to Hercules, who died from the poison of a tunic given to him by his wife. In excruciating pain, he built his own funeral pyre and ended his life in flames. The early Church Father Tertullian relates in his apologetic writings that he saw a criminal dressed up to look like Hercules, presumably with a lion's skin and club, who was burned alive in the Colosseum. That must also have been the fate of poor Meniskos. This epigram is one of the few poems of Lucillius that seems to have been based upon an actual occurrence and may have influenced Martial's early book *On the Spectacles,* which describes events in the recently completed Colosseum.

XII (AP 11.11)

When wealthy Romans went to banquets, they often brought slaves who stood at their feet and attended to them. The poet complains that Epikrates brings so many slaves that they practically constitute a Greek chorus. He refers to the slaves as "dancers," perhaps because they are so busy milling about. Though it was the custom to pass a bit of food back to the slaves so that they too could get some dinner, Epikrates overdoes it. Martial makes a similar complaint in 3.23:

> Since you pass all the dishes back
> To slaves to eat,
> Why don't we put the dining table
> At your feet?

XIII (AP 11.313)

The famine is "silver" and the plates "hungry" because the host has spent too much money on serving dishes and not enough on what he put on them. Martial, in his famous poem about the good life (10.47), also approves of a *sine arte mensa,* a table without pretension.

XIV and XV (AP 11.137 and AP 11.394)

The next two poems are about hosts too eager to read their poetry to their guests, which seems to have been a common complaint in Rome. Martial's epigram 3.50 begins,

> There is one reason why I am invited,
> Just one: so that your poems can be recited.
> As soon as I can give my shoes the toss,
> A tome's put by the salad and fish sauce.

In the first of these epigrams, Lucillius says he'd rather die than hear any more of his host's poems. The friends of Ulysses who ate the cattle belonging to Helios, the sun god, are described in book 12 of the *Odyssey*. Ulysses had been warned not to touch the cattle sacred to Helios on the island of Thrinakia; but while he was sleeping, his hungry men rounded up several animals and began to slaughter them. Zeus later punished the crew by striking the ship with lightning, and everyone but Ulysses "gulped the ocean's swell" and drowned.

XVI (AP 11.312)

The next two epigrams are about poets, again a common theme in Martial's verse. The first has been variously interpreted, but its meaning seems clear. Lucillius is making fun of a poet who built a fake tomb to show off his poetry. We are asked to weep—not "to show that the poet has indeed elicited our tears," as Rozema says, but because the poet so pretentiously attempts to draw attention to his work and the poem is so mediocre. Many commentators have observed that the Greek of the last line could also be telling the passerby to "go to the devil," but this seems to me to be irrelevant to the rest of the epigram.

XVII (AP 11.132)

"Sing, oh Goddess, wrath" comes from the first line of Homer's *Iliad*. Priam was the king of Troy. "High Zeus" is used in the poem as a synonym for "Lord Caesar," and both indicate Nero (see X and note). This epigram makes fun of the predisposition of critics to prefer the poetry of an earlier age and complains of the difficulty all young poets experience of having their work heard. Even if the poet could sing like Homer, no one would listen to him "unless, / Half-bald, as old as Priam, he'd possess / A back bent over." The last line repeats this theme: hernias were then (as now) much more common among the elderly.

XVIII – XX (AP 11.161, AP 11.159, and AP 11.164)

Many of Lucillius's epigrams make fun of people in various occupations (see the introduction to this chapter). These three epigrams satirize astrologers, who had a dubious reputation in Roman society. They were periodically banished and their practice on occasion banned, but they seem also to have been regularly consulted. Suetonius relates that when Nero was born, many astrologers made direful predictions from his horoscope. Tacitus says that Agrippina consulted astrologers about her son Nero, and when she was told that he would be emperor but would kill his mother, she is reported to have replied, "Let him kill her, provided he is emperor." Suetonius also says that near the end of his life, Nero consulted the astrologer Balbillus regarding the appearance of a comet, commonly thought to portend the death of great rulers. The prominent role astrologers played in the life of the court coupled with their uncertain status made them easy targets of lampoon. Saturn (in XVIII) was thought by the ancient Greeks and Romans to be malefic, the most unlucky of the planetary signs.

XXI (AP 11.194)

The next five poems I have selected pillory people in other occupations. This epigram about a hunter also offers Lucillius an opportunity to parody pastoral poetry. Notice how similar the beginning of this poem is to Anyte XI; it also resembles Leonidas XXV, which likewise addresses Pan and is about a hunter. But whereas Anyte and Leonidas were helping to create a new kind of poetry that appealed to the interest of Hellenistic Greeks in the simple life and the countryside, Lucillius used the conventions of this genre to debunk its idealism and sentimentality.

XXII (AP 11.249)

A farmer bought a farm said to be smaller than an atom. It is difficult to know what sort of response Lucillius expected from his readers. The situation of the farmer is pathetic, and the comparison to atoms at the end seems an easy laugh at the poor farmer's expense. The poem is nevertheless interesting for its mention of atomic theory, made famous in Rome by the Latin poet Lucretius in his poem *De Rerum Natura* (ca. 55 BCE) but little in evidence in Latin literature of the first century CE. Lucretius (following Epicurus) thought that all things were composed of atoms, which were indivisible and constituted the building blocks of the natural world. This provides the context for the hyperbole of the last couplet.

XXIII (AP 11.191)

The target is now a barber. Ares is the god of war, and the beginning of the first line, "Oh bloody Ares, man's bane," is taken word for word from the beginning of line 455 of book 5 of Homer's *Iliad*.

XXIV (AP 11.141)

Lucillius in this poem ridicules the pretentious rhetoric of the lawyer Menekles, who seems unable to get to the point but fills his speeches with irrelevant historical allusions, as if arguing a capital case in an Athenian court in the manner of a great orator like Demosthenes instead of a pleading a minor civil suit in a country town. Othryadas was a famous Spartan hero; Thermopylae, a mountain pass where a small Greek force heroically held off the whole Persian army until betrayed and slaughtered; and Xerxes, king of the Persians, whom the Greeks defeated at the battles of Salamis and Plataia. Martial used this epigram as the model for one of his poems (6.19):

Not poison, murder, beating by some brute,
But for three nanny goats I bring my suit;
A neighbor had them furtively removed,
That's what the judge is asking to be proved.
But you, with gesturing and great voice, roar
Of Carrhae and the Mithridatic War,
Of Marians and Sullans. Come now, say
How, Postumus, they took my goats away!

The allusions in Martial's poem are Roman, not Greek, and are all to defeats or disasters instead of great victories: the battle of Carrhae was a humiliating defeat for the Romans by the Parthians; the first Mithridatic War was fought with Mithridates, king of Pontus, and led to the massacre of all Romans in Asia; and the Marians and Sullans were two factions vying for power in Rome who fought a bitter civil war. The rest of the poem is nearly identical in subject and structure to Lucillius's.

XXV (AP 11.139)

Grammarians are the butt of Lucillius's wit in several poems. This is I think the best, with puns that by good fortune translate almost perfectly into English.

XXVI and XXVII (AP 11.192 and AP 11.391)

The next two poems are representative of the many epigrams Lucillius wrote at the expense of people who he and probably Nero and his court thought were disagreeable or in some way disreputable. His targets included thieves, cowards, homosexuals, cuckolds, the very lazy, and, in these two poems, people who were envious or miserly. Crucifixion was a common method of capital punishment in the Roman Empire, usually reserved for slaves and the worst sort of criminal. Tacitus says that after the conflagration in Rome, Nero, in an attempt to deflect guilt from himself, blamed the Christians, and a large number were killed, many by crucifixion. This may have provided the occasion for epigram XXVI. Epigram XXVII is clearly related to Leonidas XXVIII, in which the poet admonishes mice not to bother to look for food in his house. But though in that poem frugality is a source of pride, here it is a subject of satire.

XXVIII (AP 11.106)

The next two poems are representative of many epigrams whose subjects are people with some sort of physical defect—either they are too tall, too short, too thin, or too small, or they have very long noses. All of these poems are full of absurd exaggeration.

XXIX (AP 11.95)

Tiny Makron, whose name in Greek means "large" or "tall," throttles a mouse and lauds himself as a second Hercules, perhaps referring to a tale told of Hercules when he was an infant. Hera is said to have sent two snakes to kill him in his cradle, but Hercules strangled both of them, one with each hand, and his nurse later found him playing with their limp bodies.

XXX (AP 11.259)

This last poem is also about a physical defect but of a horse rather than a person. According to Suetonius, Nero was a great lover of horses and chariot racing from a young age. He competed in chariot racing in many places, and contrary to the usual practice, he drove the chariot himself. Suetonius says that Nero was thrown from his chariot at Olympia and couldn't finish the race but was nevertheless awarded first prize. Given the emperor's fascination with horses, this epigram would have found a receptive audience. Thessaly in the north of the Greek mainland was famous for its horses and reputed to have fielded the best cavalry in ancient Greece. This region was also renowned for magic and drugs with magical powers. Horace in *Odes* 1.27 asks of a boy in love, "What enchantress, what magician with Thessalian drugs could release you?" Thessalian witches were reputed in antiquity to have been able to draw the moon down from the sky. The Scæan or West Gate of Troy, often mentioned in the *Iliad,* was the gate through which the Trojans passed to and from the battlefield. It was also the gate the Trojan horse entered. At the end of XXX, Lucillius advises Erasistratos to use the barley from the horse's feed to make a drink called a *ptisane.* This was done by pounding the barley to decorticate it and remove the husk, and then boiling the barley in water (sometimes with spices) to make a kind of gruel for children.

SELECTED BIBLIOGRAPHY

TEXTS OF POEMS (GENERAL)

Gow, A. S. F., and D. L. Page. *The Greek Anthology: Hellenistic Epigrams.* 2 vols. Cambridge, 1965. Standard edition of poems from the *Garland of Meleager;* text in Greek with commentary in English.

—————. *The Greek Anthology: The Garland of Philip and Some Contemporary Epigrams.* 2 vols. Cambridge, 1968. Standard edition of poems from the *Garland of Philip;* text in Greek with translation and commentary in English.

Jay, P., ed. *The Greek Anthology and Other Ancient Epigrams.* Harmondsworth, 1981. English translations by various authors with brief notes and glossary.

Paton, W. R. *The Greek Anthology.* 5 vols. Loeb Classical Library. Cambridge,

MA, 1916. All of the poets and nearly all of the poems; text in Greek with English translation.

TEXTS OF POEMS (SINGLE POETS)

Anyte

Geoghegan, D. *Anyte: The Epigrams*. Rome, 1979. Text in Greek with commentary in English.

Asclepiades

Clack, J. *Asclepiades of Samos and Leonidas of Tarentum: The Poems*. Wauconda, IL, 1999. Text in Greek with vocabulary and notes in English.

Knauer, O. *Die Epigramme des Asklepiades von Samos*. Würzburg, 1935. Text in Greek with commentary in German.

Wallace, W., and M. Wallace, eds. *Asklepiades of Samos*. Oxford, 1941. Text in Greek; English translations by various authors with notes in English.

Callimachus

Lombardo, S., and D. Rayor. *Callimachus: Hymns, Epigrams, Select Fragments*. Baltimore, 1988. Translations and notes in English.

Nisetich, F. *The Poems of Callimachus*. Oxford, 2001. All of Callimachus including the epigrams in English translation with notes.

Pfeiffer, R. *Callimachus*. Vol. 2, *Hymni et Epigrammata*. Oxford, 1953. Text in Greek with textual notes in Latin.

Leonidas of Tarentum

Bevan, E. R. *The Poems of Leonidas of Tarentum*. Oxford, 1931. Text in Greek with translations and notes in English.

Clack, J. *Asclepiades of Samos and Leonidas of Tarentum: The Poems*. Wauconda, IL, 1999. Text in Greek with vocabulary and notes in English.

Geffcken, J. *Leonidas von Tarent. Jahrbücher für classische Philologie,* Suppl. 23. Leipzig, 1896. Text in Greek with commentary in German.

Lucillius

Nystrom, B. P. *An English Translation of the Poetry of Lucillius, a First-Century Greek Epigrammatist.* Lewiston, NY, 2004. Text in Greek with translation and notes in English.

Rozema, B. J. "Lucillius the Epigrammatist: Text and Commentary." Ph.D. diss., University of Wisconsin, 1971. Text in Greek with introduction and commentary in English. Available from ProQuest (http://proquest.umi.com/login).

Meleager

Clack, J. *Meleager: The Poems.* Wauconda, IL, 1992. Text in Greek with vocabulary and notes in English.

Whigham, P., and P. Jay. *The Poems of Meleager.* Berkeley, 1975. Text in Greek with translation in English.

Philodemos

Gigante, M. *Il libro degli epigrammi di Filodemo.* Naples, 2002. Text in Greek with translation and partial commentary in Italian.

Kaibel, G. *Philodemi Gadarensis Epigrammata.* Greifswald, 1885. Text in Greek with commentary in Latin.

Sider, D. *The Epigrams of Philodemos.* Oxford, 1997. Text in Greek with translation and commentary in English.

Posidippus

Austin, C., and G. Bastianini. *Posidippi Pellaei Quae Supersunt Omnia.* Milan, 2002. All the epigrams of Posidippus; text in Greek with English and Italian translations.

Bastianini, G., and C. Gallazzi. *Posidippo di Pella: Epigrammi.* Milan, 2001. The Milan papyrus: poems of Posidippus; text in Greek with translation and commentary in Italian.

Nisetich, F. "The Poems of Posidippus." In *The New Posidippus, A Hellenistic*

Poetry Book, ed. K. J. Gutzwiller, pp. 17–64. Oxford, 2005. English translations of poems from Austin and Bastianini with notes in English.

Theocritus

Gow, A. S. F. *Theocritus.* 2 vols. Cambridge, 1950. Greek text of poems including epigrams with translation and commentary in English.

Rossi, L. *The Epigrams Ascribed to Theocritus: A Method of Approach.* Leuven, 2001. Greek text with translation and commentary in English.

GENERAL INTRODUCTION TO HELLENISTIC GREECE AND ITS POETRY

Bulloch, A. W. "Hellenistic Poetry." In *The Cambridge History of Classical Literature,* Vol. 1, *Greek Literature,* ed. P. A. Easterling and B. M. W. Knox, pp. 541–621. Cambridge, 1985.

Burn, L. *Hellenistic Art: From Alexander the Great to Augustus.* London, 2004.

Fantuzzi, M., and R. Hunter. *Tradition and Innovation in Hellenistic Poetry.* Cambridge, 2004.

Fraser, P. M. *Ptolemaic Alexandria.* 3 vols. Oxford, 1972.

Green, P. *Alexander to Actium: The Historical Evolution of the Hellenistic Age.* Berkeley, 1990.

Gutzwiller, K. J. *A Guide to Hellenistic Literature.* Oxford, 2007.

Hutchinson, G. O. *Hellenistic Poetry.* Oxford, 1988.

Stephens, S. A. *Seeing Double: Intercultural Poetics in Ptolemaic Alexandria.* Berkeley, 2003.

Zanker, G. *Realism in Alexandrian Poetry: A Literature and Its Audience.* London, 1987.

INSCRIPTIONS

Ebert, J. *Griechische Epigramme auf Sieger an gymnischen und hippischen Agonen.* Berlin, 1972. Greek text of inscriptions for athletic victors with German translation and commentary.

Friedländer, P., and H. B. Hoffleit. *Epigrammata: Greek Inscriptions in Verse from the Beginnings to the Persian Wars.* Berkeley, 1948. Text in Greek with translation and commentary in English.

Hansen, P. A. *Carmina Epigraphica Graeca: Saeculorum VIII–V A.Chr.N.* Berlin, 1983.

———. *Carmina Epigraphica Graeca: Saeculi IV A.Chr.N.* Berlin, 1989. With the preceding entry, standard edition of Greek inscriptions through the fourth century BCE; text in Greek with notes in Latin.

Lattimore, R. A. *Themes in Greek and Latin Epitaphs.* Urbana, IL, 1962. Texts in Greek and Latin, with translation (Greek poems only) and commentary in English.

Powell, B. B. *Homer and the Origin of the Greek Alphabet.* Cambridge, 1991. Texts of earliest inscriptions in Greek, with translation and commentary in English.

LOVE EPIGRAMS

Garrison, D. H. *Mild Frenzy: A Reading of the Hellenistic Love Epigram. Hermes Einzelschriften* 41. Wiesbaden, 1978.

Giangrande, G. "Sympotic Literature and Epigram." In *L'Épigramme Grecque,* ed. A. Dihle, pp. 91–177. Fondation Hardt, Entretiens sur l'Antiquité Classique 14. Geneva, 1968.

Ludwig, D. W. "Die Kunst der Variation im hellenistischen Liebesepigramm." In *L'Épigramme Grecque,* ed. A. Dihle, pp. 299–348. Fondation Hardt, Entretiens sur l'Antiquité Classique 14. Geneva, 1968.

Tarán, S. L. *The Art of Variation in the Hellenistic Epigram.* Leiden, 1979.

HISTORY OF THE *GREEK ANTHOLOGY*

Cameron, A. *The Greek Anthology from Meleager to Planudes.* Oxford, 1993.

Gow, A. S. F. *The Greek Anthology: Sources and Ascriptions.* Society for the Promotion of Hellenic Studies, Supplementary Paper 9. London, 1958.

HELLENISTIC EPIGRAMS (GENERAL)

Bing, P. *The Well-Read Muse,* pp. 10–48. Göttingen, 1988.

Bing, P., and J. S. Bruss, eds. *Brill's Companion to Hellenistic Epigram.* Leiden, 2007.

Fraser, P. M. *Ptolemaic Alexandria,* pp. 553–617. Oxford, 1972.

Gutzwiller, K. J. *Poetic Garlands: Hellenistic Epigrams in Context.* Berkeley, 1998.

Reitzenstein, R. *Epigramm und Skolion.* Giessen, 1893.

Wilamowitz-Moellendorff, U. v. *Hellenistische Dichtung in der Zeit des Kallimachos,* 1:119–51, 169–80; 2:102–29. Berlin, 1924.

BOOKS AND ARTICLES
ON SINGLE POETS

Acosta-Hughes, B., E. Kosmetatou, and M. Baumbach, eds. *Labored in Papyrus Leaves: Perspectives on an Epigram Collection Attributed to Posidippus (P.Mil. Vogl. VIII 309).* Washington, DC, 2004.

Barnard, S. "Anyte: Poet of Children and Animals." In *Rose di Pieria,* ed. F. de Martino, pp. 165–76. Bari, 1991.

Bélis, A. "*Anthologie* XI, 78: Fourmillements musicaux sur la tête d'un boxeur." *Les Études Classiques* 58 (1990): 115–28.

Beta, S. "Lysianassa's Skills: Philodemus, *Anth. Pal.* 5.126 (= Sider 22)." *Classical Quarterly* 57 (2007): 312–14.

Bing, P. "Ergänzungsspiel in the Epigrams of Callimachus." *Antike und Abendland* 41 (1995): 115–31.

Blomqvist, J. "The Development of the Satirical Epigram in the Hellenistic Period." In *Genre in Hellenistic Poetry,* ed. M. A. Harder, R. F. Regtuit, and G. C. Wakker, pp. 45–60. Groningen, 1998.

Burnikel, W. *Untersuchungen zur Struktur des Witzepigramms bei Lukillios und Martial.* Wiesbaden, 1980.

Cameron, A. *Callimachus and His Critics.* Princeton, 1995.

———. "Two Mistresses of Ptolemy Philadelphus." *Greek, Roman and Byzantine Studies* 31 (1990): 287–311.

Gallavotti, C. "Epigrammi di Teocrito." *Bollettino dei Classici* 7 (1986): 101–23.

Gutzwiller, K. J., ed. *The New Posidippus: A Hellenistic Poetry Book.* Oxford, 2005.

———. "Meleager: From Menippean to Epigrammatist." In *Genre in Hellenistic Poetry,* ed. M. A. Harder, R. F. Regtuit, and G. C. Wakker, pp. 81–93. Groningen, 1998.

Longo, V. *L'epigramma scoptico greco.* Genoa, 1967.

Luck, G. "Die Dichterinnen der griechischen Anthologie." *Museum Helveticum* 11 (1954): 170–87.

Nisbet, G. *Greek Epigram in the Roman Empire: Martial's Forgotten Rivals.* Oxford, 2003.

Ouvré, H. *Méléagre de Gadara.* Paris, 1894.

Parsons, P. J. "Callimachus and the Hellenistic Epigram." In *Callimaque,* ed. F. Montanari and L. Lehnus, pp. 99–141. Fondation Hardt, Entretiens sur l'Antiquité Classique 48. Geneva, 2002.

Petrain, D. "ΠΡΕΣΒΥΣ. A Note on the New Posidippus (V.6–11)." *Zeitschrift für Papyrologie und Epigraphik* 140 (2002): 9–12.

Radinger, C. *Meleagros von Gadara, eine litterargeschichtliche Skizze.* Innsbruck, 1895.

Robert, L. "Dans l'Amphithéâtre et dans les jardins de Néron: Une épigramme de Lucillius." *Comptes Rendus de l'Académie des Inscriptions et Belles-Lettres* (1968): 280–88.

———. "Les épigrammes satiriques de Lucillius sur les athlètes: Parodie et réalités." In *L'Épigramme Grecque,* ed. A. Dihle, pp. 179–295. Fondation Hardt, Entretiens sur l'Antiquité Classique 14. Geneva, 1968.

Scodel, R. "A Note on Posidippus 63AB (*P. Mil. Vogl.* VIII 309 X 16–25)." *Zeitschrift für Papyrologie und Epigraphik* 142 (2003): 44.

Sider, D. "The Love Poetry of Philodemus." *American Journal of Philology* 108 (1987): 310–24.

Thomas, R. F. "'Death,' Doxography, and the 'Termerian Evil' (Philodemus, Epigr. 27 Page = A.P. 11.30)." *Classical Quarterly* 41 (1991): 130–37.

ABBREVIATIONS

AB   C. Austin and G. Bastianini, *Posidippi Pellaei Quae Supersunt Omnia* (Milan, 2002).

AP   *Anthologia Palatina*

APl   *Anthologia Planudea*

BG   *Bucolici Graeci*

CEG   P. A. Hansen, *Carmina Epigraphica Graeca* (Berlin, 1983, 1989).

Ebert   J. Ebert, *Griechische Epigramme auf Sieger an gymnischen und hippischen Agonen* (Berlin, 1972).

FH   P. Friedländer and H. B. Hoffleit, *Epigrammata:. Greek Inscriptions in Verse from the Beginnings to the Persian Wars* (Berkeley, 1948).

GP   A. S. F. Gow and D. L. Page, *The Greek Anthology. Hellenistic Epigrams,* vol. 1 (Cambridge, 1965), for every poet but Philodemos. For Philodemos, A. S. F. Gow and D. L. Page, *The Greek Anthology. The Garland of Philip and Some Contemporary Epigrams,* vol. 1 (Cambridge, 1968).

Pf   R. Pfeiffer, *Callimachus,* vol. 2, *Hymni et Epigrammata* (Oxford, 1953).

ILLUSTRATION CREDITS

All illustrations are by Margery J. Fain.

INDEX
OF FIRST LINES

Before five times and even nine (Philodemos XX)   195
Bittó and Nánnion are two (Asclepiades IX)   79
Bold siphons of the blood of men (Meleager XIX)   169
Bring lightning, thunder, hail and snow (Asclepiades XII)   80
But Ménippos, I know my purse is bare (Callimachus XXIV)   130
By holy Demeter, the famed Nikó (Asclepiades XVI)   81

Chairémon, lighter than (Lucillius XXVIII)   219
Cold water from two rocks cascading out (Leonidas XX)   57
Cupid brought a pleasant dream to me (Meleager XIII)   167

Deft Théris, dexterous of hand, presented (Leonidas XVI)   55
Demó is killing me, and Thérmion too (Philodemos II)   189
Didýme's bloom has put me in her power (Asclepiades XVII)   81
Do come, Eileíthyia, to her yet again (Callimachus XIV)   127
Do not, when you go sailing overseas (Leonidas III)   51
Don't bless my grave, find something else to do (Callimachus VIII)   126
Don't think your specious tears lead me astray (Posidippus VII)   96
Don't waste away by dragging out the year (Leonidas XXVII)   59
Dórkion wants to set young men on fire (Asclepiades VIII)   79
Down to the shore this crystal rock of gray (Posidippus XX)   100
Drink up, Asclepiádes, why these tears (Asclepiades XX)   82

Eight cubits keep away, inclement sea (Asclepiades I)   77
Euaínetos has dedicated me (Callimachus XVII)   128

Fish pirate, seiner, thrice-old Theris, who (Leonidas IV)   51
Flee from my cabin, dark-abiding mice (Leonidas XXVIII)   60
Fleet messenger, mosquito, fly (Meleager XXI)   170
For sailing it's the hour (Leonidas XXIX)   60
Friend, rest your weary limbs beneath this peak (Anyte XV)   41
From Leonídas, homeless and hard-pressed (Leonidas XIV)   55
From this hill, with its panoramic view (Posidippus XXVI)   102

Give her, Dorkás, this message; say (Meleager XXVI)   172

Half of my soul's still living, but the rest (Callimachus XXII)   129
Hang here, my garlands, by the double door (Asclepiades XIII)   80
Happily down the road to Hades go (Leonidas XI)   54
He offered me to you (Callimachus XVIII)   128
Hello there. "And hello to you." Your name (Philodemos XIII)   192
Here Deinoménes on this wall put me (Leonidas XXX)   60
Here Maronís, wine-lover, lies (Leonidas VI)   52

Text:	11/15 Granjon
Display:	Granjon
Compositor:	BookMatters, Berkeley
Printer:	Maple-Vail Book Manufacturing Group